7066

German Leichte Panzer at War

Text by Frank V. De Sisto
Illustrations by Laurent Lecocq

D1211620

Copyright © 2009
by CONCORD PUBLICATIONS CO.
10/F, B1, 603-609 Castle Peak Road
Kong Nam Industrial Building
Tsuen Wan, New Territories
Hong Kong
www.concord-publications.com

We welcome authors who can help
expand our range of books. If you
would like to submit material,
please feel free to contact us.

We are always on the look-out for new,
unpublished photos for this series.
If you have photos or slides or
information you feel may be useful to
future volumes, please send them to us
for possible future publication.
Full photo credits will be given upon
publication.

ISBN 962-361-147-1
printed in Hong Kong

With the defeat of Germany at the end of the Great War in 1918, the Treaty of Versailles mandated that her land forces be severely shrunken down to an army, the Reichsheer, of 100,000 men. Additionally (amongst other weapons systems), tanks were specifically prohibited from being produced or deployed; the only AFVs allowed were armored cars, which were to be used in an internal security role. Not surprisingly, the German government and the national defense forces, the Reichswehr, almost immediately undertook to develop tanks (or Panzer, literally "armor") in secret. Using a variety of cover names for projects, manufacturing firms chartered abroad and test facilities in the emerging Soviet Union, Germany managed to quietly side-step the treaty provisions that forbade the development and manufacture of tanks.

Concurrent with these endeavors, German military men, notably von Seekt, von Fritsch, Lutz and Guderian began the open study of, and the promulgation of, the theories and tactics for the use of large mechanized combined-arms armored formations. It was felt by the more visionary minds that such formations, closely supported by aircraft, would restore mobility to warfare, allow the quick penetration of enemy lines at the decisive point (the "Schwerpunkt"), and the destruction of his rear areas at an operational level. The more optimistic thought that these formations could also be effective at a strategic level if used properly.

Naturally enough, the tanks and support vehicles needed to equip these units had to be designed, tested, built and issued to the troops. Industrial design and manufacturing capacity had to be created and expanded. The units themselves had to be raised, organized and trained, tested, and than have the "lessons learned" incorporated into their continually-evolving development process. Light tanks were ideal in this regard being easier and cheaper to manufacture and maintain in the desired numbers. Both industry and the army could gain the needed experience to both mass-produce large quantities of more advanced tanks and to absorb them into their units. However, it is a disservice to refer to the early German leichte Panzer as merely "training" vehicles for both industry and the armed forces. The Pz.Kpfw.I Ausf.A and Ausf.B, as well as the Pz.Kpfw.II series through the Ausf.C, was armored to the same standards seen on mittlerer Panzer (medium tanks) such as the Pz.Kpfw.III Ausf.A, B, C and D and the Pz.Kpfw.IV Ausf.A. Based upon experiences on the Western Front during the Great War, where the machine-gun and rapid-fire field artillery was dominant, all indigenously-designed German Panzer were designed to resist 7.92mm armor-piercing ammunition and artillery shrapnel. Additionally, when formulating doctrine, none other than Guderian himself clearly stated that the leichte Panzer were intended for battle.

Panzerkampfwagen I (Sd.Kfz.101)

The Panzerkampfwagen I began its design life in 1930 as the Kleintraktor, with Krupp as the prime contractor for the chassis and Diamler Benz designing the superstructure and turret assemblies. Following an initial demonstration before Wa.Prw.6 (the automotive design bureau subordinated to the Waffenamt) at the end of July 1932, five 0-Serie Kleintraktor were ordered. The first production 1.Serie/La.S (Landwirtschaftlicher Schlepper) was accepted at the end of January 1934; these were eventually re-named Pz.Kpfw.I (MG) (Sd.Kfz.101) in April of 1936.

The Krupp-Traktor, or 1.Serie/La.S, was fitted with a front drive sprocket, a trailing idler wheel, four road-wheels and three return rollers. The suspension system had a coil spring for the first road-wheel, and leaf springs for the remaining wheels (the latter partly based on the British Carden-Loyd design). Tracks were of the dry pin type and consisted of 89 links. It was powered by a Krupp M305, 4-cylinder air-cooled gasoline engine producing 60hp. It weighed 4 metric tons, had armor up to 13mm (to resist armor-piercing bullets of up to 7.92mm in caliber), and had a top speed 37.5km/hr. Initially, no turret or superstructure was fitted. Eventually, Diamler-Benz manufactured a small series of trial superstructures and turrets, which were fitted to the 1.Serie/La.S chassis.

The 2.Serie/La.S (Panzerkampfwagen I Ausf.A) had a reinforced first road-wheel on each side. The engine deck featured 2 fuel filler caps, while the newly-introduced production-standard superstructure was fitted. For communications, an Fu.2 radio (receiver only) was fitted internally to the right of the driver; its rod antenna was mounted low on the starboard face of the superstructure. The turret was off-set to the starboard side of the superstructure roof plate and housed the commander/gunner, while to port a two-part hatch lid was provided for the driver/radio operator; one lid was mounted on the adjoining superstructure side plate. A pair of long-barreled 7.92mm MG13 machine-guns was fitted in the fully-rotating production-standard turret. The commander had four view-ports spaced around the horse-shoe shaped turret side walls, each backed by armored glass blocks. The roof plate of the turret had a half-moon shaped hatch for the commander; a signal port flap was fitted on the starboard edge of the lid. There were two hinged vision flaps on the gun mantle as well as an opening for the main armament's T.Z.F.2 telescopic sight.

As production proceeded, contracts were extended and modifications to the Pz.Kpfw.I Ausf.A were made on the assembly lines. The 3.Serie/La.S mounted shorter MG13k machine-guns, had appliqué armor plates bolted on to the superstructure sides above the track-guards, and had all road-wheels reinforced. The locations of tools and other external stowage items were modified, and the tail-lamp was replaced by a brake-lamp. The 4.Serie/La.S featured a transmission access hatch lid that was widened to 750mm, improved coil springs and shock absorbers on the first road-wheels, four fuel filler caps on the engine deck, and a re-designed horn. Modifications added later in the field or during production could include new wheels and tracks, armored guards over the engine deck air intake and exhaust grills, the fitting of a Nebelkerzenabwurfvorrichtung (rack to deploy smoke candles) on the rear plate, and the addition of a Notek black-out driving head-lamp and its associated convoy distance-keeping tail-lamp, mounted on the port side track-guard.

A more radical re-design of the Pz.Kpfw.I resulted in the introduction of the 5a.Serie/La.S, or Panzerkampfwagen I Ausf.B into production. A larger Maybach NL38TR, 6-cylinder engine generating 100hp was now fitted. The vehicle length was increased to 4.42-meters, and the weight was increased to 5.8-metric tons; the thickest armor was 15mm. The new engine and lengthened hull necessitated a change in the suspension system. This now consisted of five instead of four road-wheels, four instead of three return rollers and a new, non-trailing idler wheel; track links now numbered 100. While the superstructure remained virtually un-changed, a completely new, longer engine deck was fitted that had a revised access hatch/cooling grill arrangement. A single exhaust muffler was fitted to the rear plate, replacing the two mufflers (one on each track-guard) as seen on the Ausf.A. The turret featured a modified method of fitting internal components while the lift hooks were relocated from the side walls to the roof plate. The 6a.Serie/La.S (Pz.Kpfw.I Ausf.B) featured a reinforcing pipe for the idler wheel mounts fitted across the lower part of the hull rear plate and a modified driver's visor. Track pin return plates were mounted on the hull side walls, back near the idler wheels and new hinged mud-flaps were mounted on the rear edges of the track-guards.

Modifications to the Pz.Kpfw.I Ausf B after issue included a turnbuckle to reinforce the hull's rear plate, new vents and armored covers on the engine deck access hatch lids to provide increased power-plant cooling for Tropen (tropical) service, a Nebelkerzenabwurfvorrichtung (rack to deploy smoke candles) on the hull's rear plate, and a Notek black-out driving head-lamp mounted on the port side track-guard at the front end, along with its associated convoy distance-keeping tail-lamp at the rear end.

While the Polish Campaign was raging in the east, the first of the VK 6.01 chassis were being tested; this eventually resulted in the production of the Panzerkampfwagen I Ausf.C. In a total departure from previous models, the Ausf.C had torsion bar suspension and five pairs of interleaved road-wheels. There were no return rollers, the drive sprocket was forward-mounted and the idler wheel was mounted aft. Initially tracks were the lubricated rubber padded type, but were eventually superseded by all-steel dry-pin types. Its heaviest armor was 30mm as seen on its bow, superstructure front, turret front and gun mantle. The main armament was the 7.92mm EW141, which fired tungsten-cored armor-piercing projectiles in the classic semi-automatic mode; a 7.92mm MG34 machine-gun was mounted co-axially with it. Weight was 8 metric tons, and it was powered by a Maybach HL45P, 6-cylinder water-cooled gasoline that produced 150hp. Speed on roads was an astounding (for the time) 79km/hr, while range was 300km.

While German Panzertruppen were engaged in the battles for France and the Low Countries, the first VK 18.01 (Pz.Kpfw.I Ausf.F) was completed. By this time in the war, it should have been realized that a Panzer mounting only two 7.92mm MG34 was hopelessly inadequate, despite armor of up to 80mm in thickness. The Panzer ran on torsion bar suspension featuring five interleaved pairs of road-wheels, no return rollers, a forward-mounted drive sprocket and a rear-mounted idler wheel. These ran on all-steel dry-pin tracks. Power was provided by a Maybach HL45P 6-cylinder water-cooled gasoline engine that produced 150hp; this allowed a maximum speed on roads of 25km/hr. This "leichte" Panzer now weighed 21 metric tons, which was almost as much as the standard mittlerer Panzer, the Pz.Kpfw.IV.

The key to German Panzertaktik was command, control and communications using wireless radio transmission. To fulfill this task, an armored command vehicle, the kleine Panzerbefehlswagen I (Sd.Kfz.265) was built on both the Ausf.A and Ausf.B hull. It carried Fu.2 and Fu.6 radio transmitters and receivers and now had a three-man crew. It was armed with one 7.92mm MG34 in ball mount on the casemate front plate, while its weight increased to 5.88 metric tons. Originally, these leichte (Funk) Panzerwagen were built on the Pz.Kpfw.I Ausf.A hull and superstructure, which had an extended cupola with flush-mounted hatch lids for the commander added over the location that formerly housed the turret. The production kl.Pz.Bef.Wg. was built in three styles: 1.Serie, 2.Serie and 3.Serie. The 1.Serie/kl.Pz.Bef.Wg. was based on a modified Ausf.A hull with a suspension system like the Ausf.B, to include an added non-trailing idler wheel, four return rollers and five road-wheels. It had no cupola on top of its full-width raised superstructure, only a hatch with split lids. The 2.Serie/kl.Pz.Bef.Wg. was built on a standard Ausf.B hull as was the 3.Serie/kl.Pz.Bef.Wg. Each of these latter types could be retro-fitted with one of two styles of fixed commander's cupola. Modifications seen after production on the Pz.Kpfw.I Ausf.B were also seen on the kl.Pz.Bef.Wg. Photos exist showing 15mm Zusatzpanzer (appliqué armor) plates bolted to the bow, cupola front and superstructure front, as well as a 12mm plate on the upper glacis.

Another important variant was the Schulfahrzeuge Ausf.A and Ausf.B; these were driver training vehicles. The initial type, called the Umbau-Fahrzeuge was a 1.Serie/La.S that had never been fitted with armored superstructures and turrets. The so-called Schulfahrzeuge was based on 5b/La.S chassis (Pz.Kpfw.I Ausf.B) without the armored superstructure or turret; sheet metal enclosed the engine compartment. The Umsetz-Fahrzeuge built on 7c.Serie/La.S and 8c.Serie/La.S chassis' was fitted with items that would allow its conversion to a battle tank and included an armored engine compartment. Pz.Kpfw.I Ausf.A chassis that were converted to Schulfahrzeuge by user units could have their turrets and superstructure transferred to the Umsetz-Fahrzeuge to create battle-worthy Pz.Kpfw.I Ausf.Bs.

Other variations constructed on Panzerkampfwagen I chassis included the following: Brückenleger (bridge-layer); Instandsetzungskraftwagen (tracked vehicle for transporting maintenance equipment); Ladungsleger (demolition charge-layer) and the improved type fitted with Abwurfvorrichtungen (explosive charge dropping device). An ambulance as well as a Munitionsschlepper (armored ammunition carrier) was also produced based on redundant chassis; re-conditioned turrets from such converted leichte Panzer were ground-mounted as part of fixed fortifications.

Panzerkampfwagen II (Sd.Kfz.121)

The first 1.Serie/La.S 100 (Panzerkampfwagen II) was produced in 1936, following a request for a design that was issued in 1934, and was immediately introduced into service. Of the first 75 Pz.Kpfw.II produced, 25 each were designated Ausf.a/1, a/2 and a/3. The second pre-production group, the 2.Serie/La.S 100 saw 25 more completed by March of 1937. Characteristics common to all of these developmental models was a suspension system that consisted of three pairs of small road-wheels supported by leaf spring bundles, with the whole reinforced by a steel girder. There were three return rollers, a front-mounted drive sprocket and a rear-mounted idler wheel, all of which drove a dry-pin all-steel track. The Ausf.b introduced a new engine and various small changes were made to the engine deck and suspension system.

The Pz.Kpfw.II Ausf.c (2 and 3.Serie/La.S 100) was the final developmental version and was armored up to 13mm like its predecessors. Its major change was the suspension system, which now had five larger road-wheels, each with its own spring bundle. There were now four return rollers instead of the three previously seen. The Ausf.A (4.Serie/La.S 100), Ausf.B (5.Serie/La.S 100) and Ausf.C (6.Serie/La.S 100) introduced increased armor up to 14.5mm on the frontal arc, with 16mm on the gun mantle. Due to combat experiences in Poland in 1939, an additional 20mm Zusatzpanzerung (appliqué armor) plate was bolted to the turret and superstructure, while Vorpanzer (spaced armor) was fitted over the hull front, with the majority of these leichte Panzer so fitted by the start of the French Campaign in 1940. Eventually they were also retro-fitted with a commander's cupola with all around vision provided by periscopes; this replaced the original split-hatch lids.

The Pz.Kpfw.II Ausf.D and the Pz.Kpfw.II Ausf.E (8.Serie/La.S 138) was conceived to provide reconnaissance units with a faster leichte Panzer. To this end these two models featured torsion bar suspension with four road-wheels per side and were armored up to 30mm. These saw little action as gun tanks and prior to the French Campaign in 1940, they were taken out of front-line service to be converted into Flammpanzer (flame-throwing tanks).

The ultimate version of the Pz.Kpfw.II was the Ausf.F (9.Serie/La.S 100). It rode on the same suspension system used on the Ausf.A to Ausf.C. It was armored up to 35mm and replaced the rounded bow of its predecessors with a flat plate; likewise, the superstructure front plate was now straight instead of being bent. The driver had a visor similar to that fitted to German mittlerer Panzer such as the Pz.Kpfw.III and Pz.Kpfw.IV; to its right was a false one made from aluminum. As with its previous stable-mates, the Ausf.F had a three-man crew that consisted of a commander/gunner, radio operator and driver, while the turret still retained the 2cm KwK30 auto-cannon and co-axial 7.92mm MG34 machine-gun. It weighed 9.5 tons, was 4.81-meters long, 2.28-meters wide and 2.15-meters high. Its Maybach HL62TR engine gave it a top speed on roads of 40km/hr and a range of 200km. It was fitted with a Fu.5 radio transmitter/receiver.

Modifications seen after production included the fitting of a Nebelkerzenabwurfvorrichtung (rack to deploy smoke candles) on the rear plate and a Notek black-out driving head-lamp mounted on the port side track-guard at the front end, along with its associated convoy distance-keeping tail-lamp at the rear end.

Efforts to improve the mobility of the basic leichte Panzer in the reconnaissance role resulted in the production of several new versions of the Pz.Kpfw.II. These included the Ausf.G (VK 901), Ausf. H and the similar Ausf.M (both designated VK 903), as well as the Ausf.J (VK 1601), which were characterized by having torsion bar suspension with five pairs of interleaved road-wheels; the Ausf.J had armor up to 80mm. Limited numbers were produced and issued to field units.

The final variation of the Panzerkampfwagen II to see actual combat was the Ausf.L (VK 1303), Sd.Kfz.123, also known as the "Lüchs" (Lynx). It was to be used as a Panzerspähwagen (armored reconnaissance vehicle) and was fitted with torsion bar suspension with five pairs of interleaved road-wheels on each side, which ran on dry-pin all-steel tracks. It had a four-man crew consisting of the commander, gunner, driver and radio operator. Weighing 11.8 metric tons, it was 4.63-meters long, 2.48-meters wide and 2.21-meters high. Its Maybach HL66P gasoline engine developed 180hp, which drove it to 60km/hr on roads out to a range of 260km. Armor was up to 30mm on the frontal arc and the armament was the 2cm KwK38 auto-cannon with a co-axial 7.92mm MG34. The basic radio was the Fu.Spr.Ger.f, while command vehicles were fitted with the longer-ranged Fu.12; the latter were characterized by the addition of a pivoting Sternantenne D (star aerial). During its production run the Lüchs had several modifications made. These included a the addition and then deletion of a pair of triple-tube Nebelkerzenwurfgeräten (one on each side of the turret), addition of a Fuchsgeräte (engine coolant heater), deletion of the driver's K.F.F.2 periscopes, replacement of the steering unit, and deleting one Bosch black-out driving head-lamp from the starboard-side track-guard. Several details were changed on the turret during production to include the rear access hatch and lid, while user units extensively modified the external stowage arrangements.

Variations of the basic Pz.Kpfw.II included: Panzerkampfwagen II Flamm Ausf.A and Ausf.B (Sd.Kfz.122) (flame-thrower tank) based on Ausf.D and E chassis, respectively; Pz.Kpfw.II mit Schwimmkörper (amphibious tank); Brückenleger (bridge-layer); Munitionsschlepper (ammunition carrier); Pionier-Kampfwagen (engineer equipment tank) and Ambulance. Redundant turrets from these conversions were mounted on fixed fortifications.

Panzerkampfwagen 35(t)

In one of his bold, early conquests, Adolf Hitler's Nazi Germany, with the complicity of the rest of Europe at Munich, dismembered and then absorbed the remaining bits of Czechoslovakia into the Third Reich. In doing so Hitler gained several advantages. His ability to strike to the east and south-east was enhanced; he gained access to a large quantity of modern weaponry including tanks, other AFVs, ordnance and small arms; he gained control of the extant and relatively modern arms production industry and used it aggressively; he gained natural resources and an initially pliable population; finally, he did not have to do battle with the willing and able Czechs.

The famed Skoda firm had developed the S-II-a/LT.vz.35 light tank for a Czech Army specification issued at the end of 1934, with a prototype fielded in the summer of 1935. 298 were ordered by mid-June 1936, with the first one accepted in December 1936; approximately half of the order was constructed by cartel member CKD. Production was not continued after the occupation, with a total of 244 confiscated by the Germans.

Armament consisted of a 3.7cm KwK.M.34 main gun with a co-axial

7.92mm MG35(t) or MG37(t); a similar weapon was mounted on the superstructure front plate for use by the radio-operator. German-fielded Pz.Kpfw.35(t) had a four-man crew, versus the original three men as designed. These were: the commander/gunner, loader, radio operator and driver; the loader was added to relieve the already overworked commander of that duty. With a length of 4.9-meters, a width of 2.055-meters and a height of 2.37-meters, the combat weight was 10.5 metric tons; armor was up to 25mm. The power plant was a Skoda Model S IIa, 4-cylinder, water-cooled gasoline engine, producing 120 HP. Maximum speed on roads was 34km, with a range of 190km. The suspension was based on the British Vickers design, using leaf springs, with two clusters of four wheels each, one un-sprung wheel up front, four return rollers, a drive sprocket and an idler wheel. The vehicle ran on dry-pin, all-steel track. Eventually designated the Pz.Kpfw.35(t), this leichte Panzer was used by the German Army to supplement their Panzertruppen establishment prior to the invasion of Poland. Armed with an effective 3.7cm gun, they were used as surrogate mittlerer Panzer due to production shortfalls in Germany's indigenously-designed Panzerkampfwagen III.

Surviving Pz.Kpfw.35(t)s were re-built at Skoda after the Polish Campaign. These had revised external stowage arrangements and other German items added, including a Notek black-out driving head-lamp and rear convoy tail-lamp, Antennafuß (flexible rubber antenna base) and Stabantenne (rod antenna) on the port front corner of the superstructure and a Nebelkerzenabwurfvorrichtung (rack to deploy smoke candles).

The standard Pz.Kpfw.35(t) was fitted with an Fu.2 radio receiver; it could not transmit. Zugführer (platoon commanders) vehicles were fitted with an Fu.5 transmitter and receiver set. Kompanie-Führer (company commanders) vehicles mounted an Fu.2 and Fu.5; in these cases, the main armament remained intact and operational, whereas the radio operator's MG37(t) was deleted, with the opening plated over. The Abteilung-Kommandeur (battalion commanders) also had the Fu.5 and Fu.2 in their Sd.Kfz.266. The gross Panzerbefehlswagen (Sd.Kfz.267) mounted the Fu.5 and Fu.8 radio systems for use by the Regiments-Stab (regimental headquarters); this type was fitted with a Rahmenantenna (frame antenna) and a dummy 3.7cm KwK.

The only main variant was the Artillerie Schlepper 35(t), which was used as a prime mover. At least one dozen surviving Pz.Kpfw.35(t) chassis had their turrets removed (the area was given a frame and a canvas foul weather tarp) and an enlarged tow hook added at the rear for hauling heavy artillery in the 12-ton class. Redundant turrets were fitted to fixed fortifications.

Panzerkampfwagen 38(t)

What eventually came to be known as the Pz.Kpfw.38(t) was designed by CKD (Ceskomoravska-Kolben-Danek) as the TNH-S light tank. The prototype was delivered in January 1938 as the TNH-S and accepted for production in August of that year, with 150 planned. The first ten LT vz.38 were accepted by Germany, from the re-named BMM, or Böhmisch-Mährische Maschinenfabrik, in May of 1939. Used as a substitute for the Pz.Kpfw.III, this leichte Panzer carried various designations until June of 1940, when it was called Panzerkampfwagen 38(t).

Armament consisted of a single 3.7cm KwK38(t) with a co-axial 7.92mm MG37(t); a second machine-gun was located on the front superstructure plate. The crew consisted of four men: commander/gunner, loader, radio operator and driver; the Germans added the loader to relieve the already overworked commander of that duty. This leichte Panzer had a length of 4.9-meters, a width of 2.055-meters and a height of 2.37-meters; it had a combat weight of 10.5 metric tons. It was powered by a Praga Typ TNHPS/II 6-cylinder, water-cooled gasoline engine, which developed 125hp; this provided for a maximum speed on roads of 34km/hr, with a range on roads of 190km. The suspension consisted of leaf springs in two clusters, with two wheels each, on each side of the hull. A front-mounted drive sprocket, a rear idler wheel and two return rollers completed the system which ran on dry-pin all-steel track. Armor thickness varied from 25mm to 50mm depending on the version; basic platoon tanks were equipped with an Fu.2 radio (receiver only).

The Pz.Kpfw.38(t) Ausf.A was essentially the original Czech version and was distinguished by the initial road-wheels with narrow tire. It had the original tubular battle aerial, MG37(t) machine-guns without flash suppressors and the initial commander's periscope. The Ausf.B had the following modifications. An armored cap was fitted to the commander's periscope and both MG37(t)s had flash suppressors added; the co-axial MG was fitted with an external traverse limiting plate and a rain guard was fitted over the opening for the gun sight. Rhomboid-shaped Tac number plates were added in three locations (port and starboard track-guards, rear plate) and boarding assist handles were added to the superstructure and turret roof plates. A Notek black-out driving head-lamp, convoy distance-keeping and brake tail-lamps was fitted and wider rubber tires with thinner steel bands comprised the road-wheels. The Ausf.C had its hull front armor increased to 40mm and a bump-stop mounted near the first road-wheel station. The Ausf.D featured an armored turret ring guard, and a German style flexible rubber Antennafuß (antenna base) with a mounting bracket (both of which could be retro-fitted to earlier models).

The Pz.Kpfw.38(t) Ausf.E had its armor increased with a 25mm Zusatzpanzerung (appliqué armor) fitted to the turret, hull and superstructure front plates. The angle between the first two hull side armor plates was altered to coincide with the new straight superstructure front plate. 15mm Zustazpanzerung was fitted to the superstructure sides, while the turret sides, roof and rear plates were also thickened. The turret ring's armored guard's diameter was enlarged and new cast visors were introduced for the radio-operator and driver; armored caps for starter crank opening and track tension adjustment mechanism covers were added on the rear plate. The Ausf.F had the engine's exhaust muffler position raised in order to accommodate an armored smoke candle dispenser. A new tow coupling was fitted on the rear plate for use in hauling a fuel trailer. The Ausf.G featured 50mm-thick homogenous plates on hull, superstructure and turret fronts. A sliding cover for the engine air intake grill was added, while the Notek black-out driving head-lamp was relocated from the port track-guard to the bow plate.

The Pz.Kpfw.38(t) Ausf.S was an order for Sweden that was confiscated by Germany. It had armor 25mm thick, plus 25mm Zusatzpanzerung fitted to turret, hull and straight superstructure front plate, while the driver's and radio operator's visors as well as turret ring guard were of the type seen on the Ausf.D. The remaining features are otherwise similar to the Ausf.E.

Modifications seen after production included the fitting of a Nebelkerzenabwurfvorrichtung (rack to deploy smoke candles) on the rear plate, additional Gepäckkasten (baggage bins) on the track-guards and a Notek black-out driving head-lamp mounted on the port side track-guard at the front end, along with its associated convoy distance-keeping tail-lamp at the rear end.

The standard Pz.Kpfw.38(t) was fitted with an Fu.2 radio receiver; it could not transmit. Zugführer (platoon commanders) vehicles were fitted with an Fu.5 transmitter and receiver set. Kompanie-Führer (company commanders) vehicles mounted an Fu.2 and Fu.5. In these cases, the main armament remained intact and operational, whereas the radio opearter's MG37(t) was deleted, with the opening plated over. The Panzerbefehlswagen (Sd.Kfz.266, 267 and 268) were allotted and equipped as follows: Abteilung-Kommandeur (battalion commanders,

Sd.Kfz.266) mounted the Fu.5 and Fu.2. The Sd.Kfz.267 mounted the Fu.5 and Fu.8 radio systems for use by the Regiment-Stab (regimental headquarters) and Panzerfunkkompnie; it was these versions only that carried the characteristic Rahmenantenne (frame antenna) and that had their main armament removed and replaced with a dummy gun tube.

Conclusions

Germany's introduction of indigenously-designed and manufactured leichte Panzer into their battle order conferred several advantages, the main one being the restoration of mobility to the battlefield. These vehicles were indeed intended for combat and that they performed well in the early campaigns despite inadequate armor and armament is more a testament to German tactics than to any surmised technical superiority. Circumstances proved that the Pz.Kpfw.I and Pz.Kpfw.II were the right tanks at the right time in spite of their obsolescence. Later on, various leichte Panzer were used as a reconnaissance vehicle, which was a far more suitable role for the type, given the evolution of other nations' contemporary tanks.

The timely introduction of the Pz.Kpfw.35(t) and Pz.Kpfw.38(t) into Germany's inventory allowed the Heer to flesh-out several Panzer-Divisionen with surrogate mittlerer Panzer. By far the greatest contribution Czech industry made to long-term German aims was the use of the Pz.Kpfw.38(t) chassis for the production of a wide variety of self-propelled gun mounts as well as a light reconnaissance tank. These included the mounting of 2cm Flak and KwK, 7.62cm and 7.5cm PaK and 15cm guns on variations that included a revised, mid-engine hull. When Sturmgeschütz III production was disrupted by Allied air raids on manufacturing centers, the Jagdpanzer 38(t) was born, based on components of the Pz.Kpfw.38(t).

References

The base reference for this book is the classic "Encyclopedia of German Tanks of World War Two, Revised Edition", by Chamberlain, Doyle and Jentz. It is supplemented by the up-dated material found in the Panzer Tracts series, specifically Numbers 1-1, 1-2, 2-2, 18 and 19-1, by Jentz, Doyle and Regenberg. Material on the Czech Panzer was gleaned from the MBI books "Praga LT vz.38/ Pz.Kpfw.38(t)" and "Skoda LT vz.35", by Kliment and Francev. Further information was found in their two other books on the subject of Czechoslovak AFVs, "Czechoslovak Armored Fighting Vehicles 1918-1948" and "Czechoslovak Armored Fighting Vehicles 1918-1945". Nuts & Bolts Vol.11, Panzerkapmfwagen 35(t) (Skoda LT vz.35), by Rue, was consulted for additional information. Organizational information came from "Panzer Truppen 1" by Jentz and "Panzer Divisions of World War Two" by Crow and Watkins. A new source of pre-war and early war Panzer development and employment is the Panzerwaffe series of books: Volume 1 "The Evolution of the Panzerwaffe to the Fall of Poland 1939", by the team of Prigent, Strasheim, Jurado, Franco and Russ, and Volume 2 "The Campaigns in the West 1940", by Healey; both helped with additional pieces of the puzzle. Colors and marking information came from Zaloga's "Blitzkrieg, Armor Camouflage and Markings 1939-1940" as well as his "The Eastern Front, Armor Camouflage and Markings 1941-1945", supplemented by new information in the previously cited Panzer Tracts and Panzerwaffe volumes.

Acknowledgements

The author wishes to extend his sincere thanks to the authors, artists and researchers cited above, for their years of work to clarify the subject of German AFVs, particularly the lighter types. Thanks must also go to my partner in this latest endeavor (our tenth as a team), Laurent Lecocq. His continuing support is as always, most appreciated. A data base of German terms was reviewed for spelling by Ralph Zwilling, for which he has my eternal thanks. Finally, thanks must again go to Freddie Leung and the team at Concord for uncovering yet more new and interesting images. Any errors of fact are the sole responsibility of the author.

In a move typically reserved for the Propaganda-Kompanie photographer, an Umbau-Fahrzeuge slams into a tree prior to knocking it down. In a combat situation, this would not be a good idea since the belly plate scraping over the tree-stump could cause the suspension system to lose traction, possibly immobilizing the Panzer at a very in-opportune moment. Of interest is the way the suspension system articulates over the rough ground; note also the configuration of the safety railing in front of the crew compartment, which differs from that seen in the left two photographs.

These two photographs depict the same Umbau-Fahrzeuge as it climbs a hill during a wartime driver training session. Note the non-standard placement of the retro-fitted Notek blackout-driving head-lamp on the glacis plate, as well as the tow cable stowage. The usual "Fahrschule" (driver's school) sign is affixed to the safety railing in front of the open crew compartment, while there appears to be a two-tone camouflage pattern visible on the bow plate and mud-flap.

These two mechanics are at work on their Umbau-Fahrzeuge's transmission/final drive unit. Note that they have "broken track" on both sides of the vehicle and that the transmission compartment access plate is laying on the cobblestone surface just beneath the bow. There is also a four-digit number seen on the plate as well as a two-letter prefix, possibly "Pz.", painted in white. Again, note the configuration of the safety rail around the crew compartment, the typical Fahrschule (driver's school) plate and the location of the retro-fitted Notek blackout-driving head-lamp.

Under the watchful gaze of some locals, this crew has taken their Umbau-Fahrzeuge out for a morning ride. Aside from the usual safety rail around the crew compartment, with the typical Fahrschule (driver's school) plate, the retro-fitted Notek blackout-driving head-lamp is located in the more usual position, up forward on the port-side track-guard. There is also a letter/number stenciled in white on the transmission/final drive compartment access lid, seen just below the standard covered head-lamp.

A pair of Pz.Kpfw.I Ausf.As pass through a barrier on their way up-hill at a training area. Note that the man standing on the track-guard of the near Panzer wears an armband on his great-coat; this usually denotes a position as an exercise umpire or a range safety officer. The crewman in the turret of the following Panzer also wears an armband. The lead Panzer shows traces of the three-tone "feuersicherem Buntfarbenanstrich" camouflage system on the front plate of the superstructure.

Three crewmen check the tracks on the front of their Umbau-Fahrzeuge during a drive through their training area. Of note are the two fire extinguishers fixed to the port-side track-guard. The configuration of the safety rail around the crew compartment is also unusual in that there is no opening towards the front.

Seen during one of the many pre-war propaganda spectacles held at Nuremburg, a Panzer-Kompanie consisting of Pz.Kpfw.I Ausf.As parades before the crowd. The nearest Panzer exhibits the three-tone "feuersicherem Buntfarbenanstrich" camouflage system of Nr.17 Erdgelb-matt, Nr.28 Grün-matt and Nr.18 Braun-matt sprayed on in a soft-edge pattern, dating this image as being made some time prior to July 1937.

An early version of the mittlerer Zugkraftwagen 8-ton Sd.Kfz.7 (KMm10) prepares to pull a Sd.Ah.115 trailer upon which sits a Pz.Kpfw.I Ausf.A. Note that the trailer's rear wheels have been detached, thereby allowing the Panzer to be driven or winched onto the load-bed. The three-tone "feuersicherem Buntfarbenanstrich" camouflage can be clearly seen on the half-track's canvas foul weather cover.

In a pre-war image (note the three-tone "feuersicherem Buntfarbenanstrich" camouflage on the turret of the nearest Pz.Kpfw.I Ausf.A) a Kompanie-sized group of Panzertruppen receive flowers from local women at what appears to be a Nazi party rally. Note the banners on poles in the background.

This column of Pz.Kpfw.I Ausf.As winds its way up out of a valley, probably during the late pre-war era. Note the glacis plate on the near Panzer, which clearly shows the three-tone "feuersicherem Buntfarbenanstrich" camouflage scheme to good effect; the colors have been sprayed on in a soft-edge pattern. Typical of the time period, no markings are visible.

This close-up view of the suspension of this bogged-down Pz.Kpfw.I Ausf.A underscores the reality of tracked armored vehicle operations: mobility is still limited by the type of terrain. Note that the pre-war "feuersicherem Buntfarbenanstrich" three-tone camouflage system of Nr.17 Erdgelb-matt, Nr.28 Grün-matt and Nr.18 Braun-matt, painted on in a hard-edge pattern, is clearly discernable on the superstructure side plate.

These three photos depict the same mud-covered, but otherwise non-descript Pz.Kpfw.I Ausf.A, as it stands in a field with its crew and some friends, posing for the camera. A boon to modelers, it shows both sides of the same Panzer; note that it is painted in the pre-war "feuersicherem Buntfarbenanstrich" three-tone camouflage system. Typically for a Panzer on pre-war exercises, the twin MG13k armament has not been fitted; note the tiny opening in the mantle between the gun mounts, which was used for sighting the weapons. The unusual fitting seen on the port-side track guard is in fact the standard (but in this case, in its rarely-seen empty configuration) mounting bracket for storing the vehicle's external fire extinguisher.

Surrounded by Panzertruppen, this Pz.Kpfw.I Ausf.A shows clear evidence of the pre-war "feuersicherem Buntfarbenanstrich" three-tone camouflage system on the turret side and the superstructure front plate. In this case, the MG13ks are mounted, but covered against the elements; typically, the mud-flaps have been removed to prevent unnecessary damage.

The larger part of a Panzer-Kompanie, complete with many lounging Panzertruppen, has been parked in open country, probably during field exercises. There is evidence of the "feuersicherem Buntfarbenanstrich" three-tone camouflage system to be seen on the near Panzer, which also has dust covers on its MG13ks. Note also the large round head-pad as well as the lock and latch on the open commander's hatch lid.

Possibly taken at the same time as the previous photograph, this Pz.Kpfw.I Ausf.A also shows parts of the pattern for the pre-war "feuersicherem Buntfarbenanstrich" three-tone camouflage system. As was the case with the previous Panzer, the pattern has been applied with hard-edges to the colors. Note also the absence of all mud-flaps, the open hatch lids and visors and the tow cable on the glacis plate in what was apparently the standard location for this item.

11

More dusty, muddy Pz.Kpfw I Ausf.As are parked in an open field during an exercise. Again, the "feuersicherem Buntfarbenanstrich" three-tone camouflage system is readily visible. Likewise, all MG 13ks have been removed and there are no mud-flaps mounted. The near Panzer has the extra armor plate bolted to its superstructure side, while the remaining Panzer do not have this feature.

A line-up of Pz.Kpfw.I Ausf.As is viewed by a group of curious Germen infantrymen, probably during pre-war exercises; none appear to have added armor plates on the superstructure sides. Note also that the wire cutters are stored attached to the vehicle jack on the near-side track-guards. The overall light-colored appearance of these Panzer are likely the result of road dust, not of the particular camouflage scheme.

A pair of Pz.Kpfw.I Ausf.As accompany a squad of advancing infantrymen during a public demonstration held at Nuremburg. Note the small groups of infantrymen spread out in the background, as well as what is probably a 7.5cm l.IG18 infantry gun being prepared by its crew. The Panzer are both finished in the "feuersicherem Buntfarbenanstrich" three-tone camouflage system.

What appears to be almost an entire Panzer-Kompanie has been marshaled in front of their barracks at a Kaserne. At the head of the column is what appears to be an Auto-Union Wanderer light field car, followed by a dispatch rider on his motorcycle. All crewmen wear the M1935 special Panzertruppen uniform, including the characteristic beret, which covered a padded helmet.

This overall close-up of the turret of a Pz.Kpfw.I Ausf.A (note the position of the turret lifting hooks, which were on the roof plate of the Ausf.B) shows several details to good effect. The sight aperture for the MG13ks is visible just over the barrel cooling jacket of the near weapon, while both view-port flaps are in their opened position. A curious addition is what appears to be a hinged bar on the front plate of the superstructure, whose function is unknown. The upper rim from the added superstructure side armor plate is visible at left.

As this Pz.Kpfw.I Ausf.A moves at high speed along a metalled road surface, an interesting optical illusion has been created; it seems that the track shoes have no guide horns, when in fact there were two rows, between which all wheels ran. The Panzer's main armament, a pair of 7.92mm MG13ks, are covered against road dust. Note also the very apparent two-tone camouflage scheme of Dunkelgrau Nr.46, over-sprayed with Dunkelbraun Nr.45, which is especially visible on the edges of the track-guards. Finally, this Panzer has been fitted with additional armor on either side of the superstructure; in this view, the plate can be seen just below the driver's entry hatch lids.

Some subtle details of the suspension system and underside of this Pz.Kpfw.I can be seen as it climbs a log barrier for the photographer. Note that the armor over the final drive on the bow plate is not one continuous curve; it is flat on the bottom. The details of the road-wheel rims and their webbed reinforcements can also be viewed on the first road-wheel.

An entire Panzer-Kompanie is lined up on Zug (platoon) columns while on an exercise. The lead vehicle in each column is a Fahrschulpanzer, while those that follow are Pz.Kpfw.I Ausf.Bs. In addition, each column is accompanied by a tactical transport truck, which would carry various consumable items for both Panzer and crewmen.

This Pz.Kpfw.I Ausf.A has pulled off to the side next to a bend in the road, apparently with transmission or final drive problems. Note that the tracks have been un-pinned and the drive sprocket has been removed. The white shapes on the ground at the front of the Panzer appear to be the opened lids of tool boxes.

With their Pz.Kpfw.I Ausf.As lined up in a march column, a group of Panzertruppen take a break from the heat on the road-side. Note that they have removed their tunics and berets to reveal their grey shirts and black ties; most men also have their hair cut in the typical German military fashion of the time. Bringing up the rear of the column is a Büssing NAG 4.5-ton tactical transport truck.

The crew of this Pz.Kpfw.I Ausf.A makes an observation of the ground to their front while halted next to what appears to be a stone watchtower from a bygone era. Note the white number 5 on the far corner of the superstructure's rear plate; this was typically painted temporarily on Panzer during the pre-war period when on exercises.

A column of Pz.Kpfw.I Ausf.As and Ausf.Bs raises a cloud of dust as they cross an open field. The Panzer all appear to be devoid of any markings, indicating that this is probably a pre-war photograph.

A German Heer (army) officer takes a break while perched on the engine deck of a Pz.Kpfw.I Ausf.A. This unusual view shows the curvature of the lower section of the hull rear plate, the trailer hitch with pin, as well as the bolted mounts for a tow cable. Other visible details include the rear sections of the track-guards as well as the exhaust muffler fish-tails.

A rather non-descript Pz.Kpfw.I Ausf.A speeds across some scrub-land during an exercise. The Panzer carries no visible markings and typically has the front (but not the rear) mud-flaps removed from the track-guards to prevent damage.

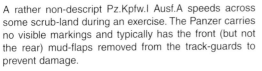

A column of Pz.Kpfw.I Ausf.As moves down the streets of a town, whose Nazi sympathies are evidenced by banners hung from buildings on either side. The scene is probably in pre-war Germany; note the nonchalant attitude of the locals on the streets.

A trio of German soldiers poses for a photograph sitting on a Pz.Kpfw.I Ausf.A. This Panzer has the additional armor plate bolted to the superstructure side, just above the track-guard. In addition both front and rear mud-flaps have been removed from the track-guards, while the pair of MG13ks has not been fitted in the turret.

It is difficult to precisely determine the model of this Pz.Kpfw.I, due to the close-cropped nature of the original image. The location of the turret lifting hooks on the roof indicates it is an Ausf.B. Note how a tow cable has been stowed on the glacis plate using the tow hooks and the head-lamp as hangers.

Having probably recently returned to their Kaserne (barracks) from field exercises, a Kompanie of Pz.Kpfw.I Ausf.A (and a Pz.Kpfw.II Ausf.a/2 or a/3, at left) waits their turn to be cleaned. In preparation for that act, the MG13ks have been removed from the turrets. Note the two-digit Tac numbers on the superstructure front plate of every Panzer; all read "65" and are either yellow, or white covered with dust.

Another scruffy group of Pz.Kpfw.I Ausf.As is lined-up in front of their storage sheds, again, probably immediately following field exercises. All have had their MG13ks removed. The first two Panzer have bolted armor strips on their superstructure sides, below the driver's access hatches; the third does not.

16

The crew of a Pz.Kpfw.I Ausf.A works on their Panzer, while a pair of locals, probably the source of the drink being held by a third soldier, stands by. This Panzer has been retrofitted with armored cowls on the rear plate and engine deck, as well as with a Nebelkerzenabwurfvorrichtung (rack to deploy smoke candles). It wears white Tac numbers, 12, on the turret in three places and is marked with a black/white Balkenkreuz low on the hull rear plate.

Moving at speed across a field, this Pz.Kpfw.I Ausf.A's tracks again display the illusion that there are no guide horns on the outside of the wheels. This very dusty Panzer has the visor above the starboard side MG13k flipped open and also has an access hatch lid on the engine deck propped in the open position. In both cases, having them open will improve cooling, but will also allow more dust to enter the interior than would normally be the case.

Although difficult to see on the original image, this Pz.Kpfw.I Ausf.A wears a white-outline rhomboid on the superstructure front plate that encloses an undecipherable letter, with a number outside of it below the left corner. Such Tac markings were typical of pre-war German Panzer that were on field exercises. This clear photograph shows many of the details of the tool stowage, various fittings, the MG13ks in the turret and the inside surfaces of the driver's access hatch lids.

While several Panzertruppen loaf and smile for the camera, one man seems to be intent on working at something just inside the driver's access hatch-way. The slight variation in tone on the front of the turret side-wall indicates that this Panzer is finished in the two-tone camouflage of Dunkelgrau Nr.46 over-sprayed with Dunkelbraun Nr.45 in patches. This rather clean Panzer is parked in front of its storage shed; it has had its MG13Ks removed for cleaning and wears a full set of mud-flaps.

As a column of trucks speeds by, a Pz.Kpfw.I Ausf.A takes a rest on the side of a road during the Polish Campaign, September 1939. Note the added armor plates on the rear deck of the engine compartment as well as the solid white Balkenkreuz national insignia on the turret. Both crewmen are visible, which means the Panzer is not moving; that, and the fact that it is alone, suggests that it has suffered a mechanical break-down and has been left behind by the rest of its unit.

A group of less-than-delighted Polish soldiers poses with the German victors, during the September 1939 conquest of that nation. Note the white Balkenkreuz and the white Tac number, 214, on the side of the turret of the nearly completely obscured Pz.Kpfw.I Ausf.A

A Pz.Kpfw.I Ausf.B is followed across a field by an Ausf.A, perhaps during the Polish Campaign of September 1939. Although neither Panzer wears the tell-tale solid white Balkenkreuz national insignia that characterized the campaign, there appears to be a three-digit Tac number in a very unusual location, on the superstructure front plate.

A group of soldiers shelters in a road-side drainage ditch as a column of wheeled vehicles is led past by a Pz.Kpfw.I Ausf.A. The Panzer shows no markings, while its crew has removed the front and rear mud-flaps from the track-guards.

18

A pair of German Heer (army) soldiers takes time from exploring this destroyed Pz.Kpfw.I Ausf.A to pose for a souvenir photograph. The Panzer has shed much of its suspension system and tracks and has suffered a rupture in the armor at the lower rear hull area. Likewise, the gun mantle and both MG13ks are missing. The Panzer has additional armor fitted to the rear deck.

On 26 October 1939, German AFVs were ordered to use a new style of Balkenkreuz national insignia. Instead of a thick, all-white marking, the new style consisted of a black center with a thin white outline. Sometimes the black center was not applied as appears to be the case here. Otherwise, this Pz.Kpfw.I Ausf.A is in the standard configuration.

Using a chain hoist attached to a log tripod, these men are apparently re-attaching the engine deck to this Pz.Kpfw.I Ausf.A, possibly during the French Campaign. A standard feature on many German Panzer was the removable engine deck/superstructure (seen on Pz.Kpfw.I, II, III and IV, as well as StuG.III), which was always bolted-on. This was a design feature needed to install and remove the engine for extensive maintenance or an exchange. Note the two-digit white Tac numbers, possibly 23, in three locations on the turret.

A pair of Pz.Kpfw.I Ausf.As leads a truck through a devastated town, probably during the French Campaign of 1940. The near Panzer clearly shows the effects that dust has in making the paint finish appear much lighter than it actually was; note the difference in tones on the bow and glacis plate. It is also a bit unusual that the second Panzer has no MG13ks fitted, although it is obviously in a combat zone.

While infantrymen and tank crewmen pose on a captured enemy bunker, probably during the French Campaign in 1940, a Pz.Kpfw.I Ausf.A is parked in the foreground. Note that the Panzer wears its front mud-flaps and mounts the later style horn on the glacis plate; additionally, the staggered arrangement of the turret's MG13ks can be easily seen.

While a Pz.Kpfw.III stands still in the background, a white-washed Pz.Kpfw.I Ausf.A moves at speed in the snow; photographs showing this type of Panzer in a winter camouflage scheme are rather rare. Note that both Panzer have Notek black-out driving head-lamps fitted, which likely places the time of the photo as after the French Campaign of May/June 1940.

Two US soldiers pose atop a Pz.Kpfw.I Ausf.A chassis that has been heavily modified to resemble a medium tank of the Pz.Kpfw.III or Pz.Kpfw.IV series. Note the thin nature of the faux superstructure as evidenced by the twisted sheet metal on the nearest AFV, and that the far AFV has a turret designed to mimic a very early mittlerer Panzer complete with a "Bishop's Miter" commander's cupola.

This column of leichte Panzer is led by a Pz.Kpfw.I Ausf.A, with retrofitted Notek black-out driving head-lamp on the port-side track-guard. What is unique about these AFVs are the markings, which most resemble those applied to Ordnungspolizei (Order Police) vehicles. There is a five-digit white registration number on the glacis plate which appears to be in two sizes, much like the Reich Interior Ministry Number applied to ORPO AFVs. The application of a Balkenkreuz on the glacis plate is also typical of vehicles assigned to these internal security (or anti-partisan) units. Finally, all vehicles have a white, single-digit Tac number on the front plate of the superstructure. Although information is incomplete, it is known that one and possibly five Pz.Kpfw.I Ausf.As were assigned to Polizei-Panzer-Kompanie 8.

A pair of Pz.Kpfw.I Ausf.Bs occupies a dirt road probably during the late pre-war period. Note the later style horn on the glacis plate next to the starboard side track-guard and the missing front mud-flaps; those at the rear are still in place. No markings are seen on these fairly dusty Panzer.

A leichte Panzer-Kompanie from the 5.Panzer-Division receives maintenance, possibly just after the conclusion of the Polish Campaign in 1939. Note the yellow and black rhomboid shapes along the lower edge of the turret of the near Pz.Kpfw.I Ausf.B, as well as the location and style of the two-digit Tac numbers, both of which were characteristics of this unit. In the background can be seen several Pz.Kpfw.IIs, which are either Ausf.As, Bs, or Cs.

The angle at which the light strikes the suspension system of this Pz.Kpfw.I Ausf.B, shows how the track's guide horns could wear the road-wheel rims down to bare metal. This leichte Panzer has a rhomboid plate attached to the near track-guard that sports a three-digit Tac number in white, possibly 405. There is some foliage placed on the engine deck to help break up the silhouette and the rod antenna is in the raised (receiving) position; radios on these early leichte Panzer could not transmit.

The location of the turret lift rings on this Pz.Kpfw.I Ausf.B suggest that it is actually a re-manufactured Umsetz-Fahrzeuge chassis that was created by taking the turret and superstructure from a converted Ausf.A Schulfahrzeuge Another characteristic of the lengthened Ausf.B hull can be clearly ascertained in this view; there were four return rollers instead of the three seen on the Ausf.A.

A group of German Panzer, including a Pz.Kpfw.I Ausf.B (nearest the camera) moves towards the enemy in a Keil (bell-shaped) battle formation. The Pz.Kpfw.I Ausf.B shows several distinguishing features of that model, including the stiffening bar that connected to the idler wheel mounts, single rear plate-mounted exhaust muffler, air vent opening on the superstructure below the turret, later convoy distance-keeping tail-lamp and relocated fire extinguisher, on the rear of the port-side track guard. Previously, the latter was mounted further forward on the Ausf.A. What are probably cells to dispense smoke candles are mounted below the exhaust muffler; these are distinctly different from those seen in most photographs. Finally, note the three-digit Tac number on the rear superstructure plate, 212.

A crewman of this Pz.Kpfw.I Ausf.B cleans an area on the engine deck with a rag while a Gebirgsjäger (mountain rifleman) looks on with some interest. Note the edelweiss insignia on the latter's Bergmütze cap and his trade badge on the left sleeve. The Panzer is fairly well covered with foliage, yet several interesting features are still visible. Note the stowage locker on the near track-guard, as well as the bundle of saplings just behind the crewman. A white-outline Balkenkreuz national insignia can be seen on the superstructure side plate below the turret, with the latter sporting a three-digit Tac number, with only a "1" distinctly visible. The form just behind the Panzer crewman is a pyramid-shaped tent made by combining four Zeltbahn rain ponchos.

The ultimate Pz.Kpfw.I was the Ausf.F, seen here deployed with Panzer-Abteilung z.b.V66 on the Ostfront in 1942. This Panzer featured interleaved road-wheels mounted on torsion bar suspension units and armor plate of up to 80mm in thickness on the bow plate, superstructure front plate and gun mantle. Rather overweight at 21 metric tons for the armament carried (2 x 7.92mm MG34s) it represented a design dead-end at a time when Germany could little afford such a luxury.

A wheeled vehicle column, most likely a divisional or regimental command unit, is led by the first main derivative of the Pz.Kpfw.I, the kleine Panzerbefehlswagen (Sd.Kfz.265). This AFV dispensed with the rotating machine-gun-armed turret for a heightened, fixed superstructure upon which was mounted an observation cupola; initial versions did not have a cupola. It was crewed by three men and carried various radios such as the Fu.2 and Fu.6.

This command element from a Panzer-Division is seen on a dusty road during the Polish Campaign of September 1939. The kl.Pz.Bef.Wg. (Sd.Kfz.265) wears the thick white Balkenkreuz national insignia on all four surfaces of the superstructure, characteristic of the campaign. Next to the AFV are a pair of BMW light field cars outfitted to carry radios; in such a configuration they were designated Kfz.22.

A pair of kl.Pz.Bef.Wg. (Sd.Kfz.265) brings up the rear of a column that includes a pair of Pz.Kpfw.IIIs, probably during the opening phases of Operation Barbarossa in June 1941. Note the spare road-wheel as well as the traces of a Tac number on the superstructure of the near Befehlspanzer as well as the huge amount of stowage items seen on all of the AFVs in this photograph.

A kl.Pz.Bef.Wg. (Sd.Kfz.265) leads another down a muddy forest path. Note the details of the welds and the hatch lid stops on the commander's cupola, as well as the engine cooling air slots cut into the access hatch lid on the rear deck of the first vehicle. The second AFV in line does not mount the MG34; its head-lamp has had its black-out driving cover removed as well.

A kl.Pz.Bef.Wg. (Sd.Kfz.265) acts as a make-shift ambulance, transporting wounded British prisoners during the French Campaign of May/June 1940. Identifying features from this angle include the opened hatch lids of the commander's cupola as well as the position of the erected rod antenna and its associated storage trough. The non-trailing idler wheel and position of the exhaust muffler identify the chassis as an Ausf.B. Note the armored Nebelkerzenabwurfvorrichtung (rack to deploy smoke candles) with black/white Balkenkreuz, at left.

The first version of the Pz.Kpfw.II was the Ausf.a/1, a/2 and a/3 (although this particular vehicle's model type is undetermined), all of which had similar features. Identifying features from this angle include the shape of the drive sprocket hub, the style of view-port covers on the turret and the suspension system with its support girder. Note the two round armored hatch lids on the superstructure side plate, aft of the turret; these covered fuel filler caps.

The three crew-members of this Pz.Kpfw.II Ausf.a/2 or a/3 take the sun on top of their Panzer in the summer of 1938. Note the graffiti on the turret and superstructure sides; the main body loosely translates as "Our work is done!" and includes the name "Mariachin" (little Maria) and the town of Wünsdorf, as well as a date, August 5, 1938. Additionally, the usual Panzer rhomboid plate is attached to the track-guard, with a white Tac number, 221 painted upon it. This Panzer is identified as an Ausf.a1 by the shape of the drive sprocket, the circular nature of the engine deck air cooling opening, the type of turret view-port flaps and the suspension system. Note also that the crewman in the turret waves a pink pennant with a black cross, whose shape indicates it is from a regiment's command section.

Probably photographed during a pre-war exercise (note the use of gas masks by the soldiers at right), a Pz.Kpfw.II Ausf.A or Ausf.B is winched aboard a Tiefladeananhäger fur Panzerkampfwagen Sd.Ah.115. Note the cable leading from the winch to the bow of the leichte Panzer and that the tracks on the near side have been removed. The frame seen on the superstructure side plate was a mount for an anti-aircraft machine-gun, which was hinged so it could swing out away from the vehicle.

A Pz.Kpfw.II Ausf.A or Ausf.B follows a Pz.Kpfw.I Ausf.A down a forest trail, probably during pre-war exercises. Note the three-digit white Tac numbers (131 and 125) seen on the turrets of both leichte Panzer; these identify the group as belonging to a Panzer-Abteilung's 1.Kompanie. The Pz.Kpfw.I has been modified with additional armored guards on the engine deck and rear plate.

This Pz.Kpfw.II shows clear evidence of the post-July 1937 two-tone camouflage scheme of Dunkelgrau Nr.46 over-painted with Dunkelbraun Nr.45, particularly on the turret side walls. Note also the Tac numbers, 711, in white as well as the absence of any armament. This leichte Panzer has disabled itself by driving into the brick wall of a building. Finally, there appears to be an attempt made at deceiving the enemy as to the exact location of the view-port on the superstructure rear plate; note the two-tone shape painted next to it.

A Pz.Kpfw.II (probably an Ausf.c as indicated by the anti-aircraft machine gun mount) lurks in a tree-line, probably during pre-war exercises; note that it does not wear any form of Balkenkreuz national insignia, which was typical for that era. A white Tac number, 211, has been painted on the superstructure side plate just behind the pivoting anti-aircraft machine-gun mount. Although this leichte Panzer is fairly dusty, evidence that it is finished in the two-tone camouflage scheme of Dunkelgrau Nr.46 over-painted with Dunkelbraun Nr.45, can be seen on the turret and the rear-most stowage locker on the near-side track-guard.

In pre-war exercises, a Pz.Kpfw.II Ausf.A or Ausf.B prepares to tow its companion through a blanket of snow. The crewmen wear their standard M1935 greatcoat over their all-black uniforms. Typical for the era, the leichte Panzer are devoid of any markings. At the estimated time this photo was taken, they would have been finished in the two-tone camouflage scheme consisting of a base of Dunkelgrau Nr.46 over-sprayed with Dunkelbraun Nr.45 in patches, so the latter color covered roughly 1/3 of the item being painted.

A trio of Pz.Kpfw.II Ausf.A, Ausf.B or Ausf.C from a Panzer-Abteilung's 5.Kompanie takes a rest during exercises. All three leichte Panzer sport rhomboid plates on their superstructure sides with three-digit Tac numbers painted on them; the first digit indicates Kompanie affiliation, the second the Zug (platoon) and the third the individual vehicle's number. Thus, the second Pz.Kpfw.II is from the Kompanie's command element.

A variety of leichte Panzer are shown in this photograph, to include two models of the Pz.Kpfw.II, as well as a pair of kl.Pz.Bef.Wg. (Sd.Kfz.265). The nearest Pz.Kpfw.II is an Ausf.A or Ausf.B, while the two further away are Ausf.a/1, a/2 or a/3s; note the differences in the suspension systems. No markings are visible other than a small, three-digit Tac number on the superstructure side plates of the Pz.Kpfw.IIs, B01, B02 and B03; these possibly identify these Panzer as belonging to a Panzer-Division's Panzer-Brigade Stabs-Truppe (brigade command group). There are rhomboid-shaped plates on the two kl.Pz.Bef.Wg., which also should have Tac numbers on them. However, the angle of the light prevents them from being read.

A group of leichte Panzer belonging to the 4.Panzer-Division takes a break in a defile, protected from prying eyes. These leichte Panzer are all marked with thick white Balkenkreuze on four positions, according to regulations promulgated in July of 1939. The kl.Pz.Bef.Wg. is marked as belonging to the Panzer-Regiment's I.Abteilung Stabs-Truppe (battalion command group), with a white "I01" on the superstructure side plate; all vehicles have a small Tac number on their superstructure front plates as well. Other items of note are the peculiar frames on the turret roof of some Pz.Kpfw.IIs (which are Ausf.As or Ausf.Bs), as well as the racks on their track-guards to carry jerry cans; there also seems to be a Fahrschulepanzer chassis bringing up the rear of the far column.

At least four Pz.Kpfw.IIs can be seen amongst this large group of wheeled vehicles, during the Polish Campaign of September, 1939. The two nearest the camera are Ausf.As or Ausf.Bs, while the one behind and between them is probably an Ausf.a/1, a/2 or a/3. Note that the thick white Balkenkreuz national insignia are only seen on the turret rear plate instead of on all four faces as per regulations. Also of note in this image is the folding rod antenna for the leichte Panzer's radio; all other contemporary German-designed Panzer had this fitting on the opposite side of the superstructure.

Seen during the Polish Campaign of September 1939, a Zug (platoon) of leichte Panzer closes in on an already burning Polish town. Note the thick all-white Balkenkreuz national insignia on the turret of the Pz.Kpfw.II in the center of the photo, a characteristic marking seen on this campaign. The Pz.Kpfw.I Ausf.A has the armored guards on the engine deck and rear plate, as well as the Nebelkerzenabwurfvorrichtung (rack to deploy smoke candles).

A Pz.Kpfw.II (probably an Ausf.A or Ausf.B) brings up the rear of a column of leichte Panzer as they make their way into a Polish city during the campaign of September 1939. Note the thick white Balkenkreuz national insignia prominently displayed on the turret walls of the Pz.Kpfw.II and the fact that there is little evidence of any extra stowage on any of the AFVs.

An armored column partially consisting of Pz.Kpfw.IIs moves down a tree-lined road, quite probably during the Polish Campaign of 1939. It would appear that the large white Balkenkreuz on the port side of the turret's rear face has been over-painted. Although the lighting makes it difficult to see, there also appears to be an intact Balkenkreuz on the turret's side wall.

A single kl.Pz.Bef.Wg. (Sd.Kfz.265) is sandwiched between a pair of Pz.Kpfw.IIs (probably Ausf.As or Ausf.Bs), during the Polish Campaign. Note the all-white Balkenkreuz national insignia on the turrets and superstructures of the Panzer in this photo; all are much smaller than was usually seen and have evidence of some sort of over-painting around their edges. The nearest Pz.Kpfw.II has a Tac number on the superstructure side plate, I45, in white; this indicates it is part of a Panzer-Regiment's I.Abteilung Stabs-Truppe (battalion command group).

Photographed amidst the ruins of a Polish city during the 1939 campaign, this knocked-out Pz.Kpfw.II Ausf.c (identified by the driver's view-port flap; a lower case letter is correct in this instance) awaits recovery. It is prominently-marked with the thick white Balkenkreuz on the front of the superstructure, while someone has removed the 7.92mm MG34 and 2cm KwK30 armament from the turret.

This Pz.Kpfw.II Ausf.A or Ausf.B stands derelict in a city after having been knocked out. The lack of any tracks or other specific vehicle-related debris indicates the Panzer was knocked out elsewhere; note also the lack of rubber on some road-wheels and return rollers. This leichte Panzer has the original two-piece split hatch lids for the commander on the turret roof; compare it to the previous image.

Although difficult to see due to the angle that light strikes the turret side wall, this Pz.Kpfw.II Ausf.A, B or C wears a white, two-digit Tac number, 42. It has some of the post-Polish Campaign modifications to include Zusatzpanzer (appliqué armor panels) on the superstructure front and the turret front, as well as Vorpanzer (spaced armor) on the bow.

With five grave markers shown, more than the three-man crew of the destroyed Pz.Kpfw.II in the background has been interred at this location. Note the road-wheels used at the grave-site as well as the Nazi flags placed on the ground.

This Pz.Kpfw.II Ausf.A, B or C has been retro-fitted with the commander's cupola that included all around vision using periscopes set about the rim; instead of large split hatch lids, it now has a smaller single circular lid. Other modifications include Zusatzpanzer (appliqué armor panels) on the superstructure front and the turret front and Vorpanzer (spaced armor) on the bow. The slightly mangled port-side track-guard has a Notek black-out driving head-lamp mounted to it; this would be accompanied by a convoy distance-keeping tail-lamp, unseen at this angle.

Quite probably photographed in the winter of 1939-1940, after the Balkenkreuz national insignia was ordered changed to the black/white style seen here, a Zug (platoon) of three Pz.Kpfw.II Ausf.A, B or C and a pair of Pz.Kpfw.Is are parked in a column in this snowy setting. Note that these 3.Kompanie leichte Panzer also carry a three-digit Tac number on a rhomboid plate attached to their superstructure sides.

This trio of Pz.Kpfw.IIs (Ausf.A, B or C) was photographed while being loaded onto (or un-loaded from) the hold of a transport ship. The Panzer at upper right carries markings identifying it as belonging to Pz.Abt.z.b.V.40, which saw action during the invasion of Norway in April of 1940. All appear to have parts of the up-grade package, including Zusatzpanzer (appliqué armor panels) on the superstructure front and the turret front and Vorpanzer (spaced armor) on the bow. A Notek black-out driving head-lamp has been mounted onto the glacis plate Vorpanzer, instead of the more common position on the port-side track-guards.

Schulfahrzeuge, Kraftfahrlehrkommando Zossen or Ohrdruf, circa 1938

In the pre-war era, these driver training tanks were in the standard color scheme of the time consisting of a base color, Dunkelgrau Nr.46 (later the code was changed to RAL 7021). This is over-sprayed with Dunkelbraun Nr.45 (later RAL 7017) in patches, so it covers roughly 1/3 of the vehicle. These vehicles lacked a superstructure and often had a rail around the crew compartment to which was fixed a simple plate describing the vehicle's function. In this case the plate is white with the inscription "Fahrschule" (literally: driving school) in black letters.

Pz.Kpfw.I Ausf.A, unidentified unit, Germany, circa 1936

Through June 1937, the so-called "feuersicherem Buntfarbenanstrich" three-tone camouflage system of Nr.17 Erdgelb-matt, Nr.28 Grün-matt and Nr.18 Braun-matt were applied to German tactical equipment, including the new Panzer. These colors could be sprayed on in a soft-edge pattern or applied with a brush in a hard-edged style. Typical of pre-war Panzer that were not on exercises, no other markings are visible.

Pz.Kpfw.I Ausf.B, Panzer-Regiment 15, 5.Panzer-Division, circa Polish Campaign, 1939
Panzer from this unit carried the distinct black and yellow rhomboid around the lower rim of the turret walls, usually in at least three places. Above these are the Tac number, a solid white 45. The base color is Dunkelgrau Nr.46. This is over-sprayed with Dunkelbraun Nr.45 in patches, so it covers roughly 1/3 of the Panzer.

Pz.Kpfw.I Ausf.A, unidentified unit, Germany, circa 1940
This Panzer is marked quite typically for a vehicle of this era, to include a large two-digit Tac number, 12, arrayed in three locations around the turret walls. A black/white Balkenkreuz national insignia can be seen low and to starboard on the hull rear plate, as well as centered on each side of the superstructure. The base color is Dunkelgrau Nr.46. This is over-sprayed with Dunkelbraun Nr.45 in patches, so it covers roughly 1/3 of the Panzer.

Kl.Bef.Pz.I Ausf.B, Panzer-Regimant 35 or 36, 4.Panzer-Division, Poland, 1939
This small command tank is marked for participation in the Polish Campaign, to include thick white Balkenkreuze (national insignia) on all four faces of the superstructure. The Tac number I01, indicates this is a battalion commander's mount; this too is seen on all four faces of the superstructure, in various sizes and locations. The division's sign, a three-pointed star is painted in yellow on the front of the superstructure, just below the Tac number. The camouflage of the period consisted of a base color of Dunkelgrau Nr.46. This is over-sprayed with Dunkelbraun Nr.45 in patches, so it covers roughly 1/3 of the Panzer.

Pz.Kpfw.I Ausf.A Munitionspanzer, Sturmgeschütz-Batterie 660, Ostfront 1941
As the Pz.Kpfw.I Ausf.A became obsolete, the chassis were used to create a variety of auxiliary vehicles, in this case an ammunition carrier for use by a Sturmgeschütz-Abteilung. A white-outline Balkenkreuze national insignia is seen on the roof hatch lids, both sides of the superstructure and on the rear plate of the hull. The unit insignia, a white-outline Maltese Cross is seen on the front and rear port-side mud-flaps. This Panzer is finished in a single color, Dunkelgrau RAL 7021.

Pz.Kpfw.II Ausf.a/2 or a/3, unidentified unit, Wünsdorf, Germany, August 1938

The crew of this Panzer have applied graffiti to the entire port side of their vehicle. It dates the photo as August 5, 1938 and gives the location as Wünsdorf. The main slogan translates as "Our work is done!", while the smaller one translates as "Little Maria". Standard rhomboid plates are seen on both track-guards as well as the rear edge of the engine deck; they are all painted with a three-digit Tac number, 221, in white. The base color is Dunkelgrau Nr.46. This is over-sprayed with Dunkelbraun Nr.45 in patches, so it covers roughly 1/3 of the Panzer.

Pz.Kpfw.II Ausf.A, B or C, 3.Kompanie, I.Abteilung, unidentified unit, Germany, circa winter of 1939-1940

This Panzer is marked with the black/white Balkenkreuz national insignia on the superstructure side plate, which is carried over on to the antenna storage trough. The three-digit Tac number, 322, is probably painted yellow; it is also on the superstructure side plate. The base color is Dunkelgrau Nr.46. This was over-sprayed with Dunkelbraun Nr.45 in patches, so it covered roughly 1/3 of the Panzer.

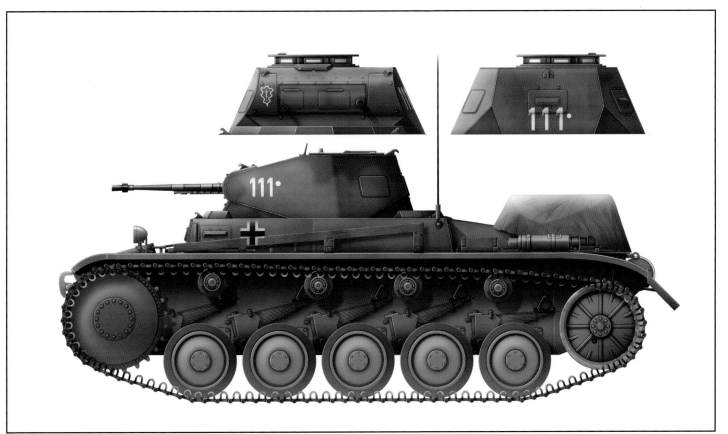

Pz.Kpfw.II Ausf.A, B or C, 1.Panzer-Division, France 1940
Uniquely, this division carried their oak-leaf insignia on the turrets of their Panzer, in this case on the starboard side of the turret face; the insignia also appeared high on the turret's rear wall. The Tac number, 111 followed by a dot is painted in white; it too would be repeated on the rear wall, low to the port side. The black/white Balkenkreuz national insignia is seen on both sides of the superstructure; on the port side it would be carried over to the antenna stowage trough. The base color of German equipment at this time period is Dunkelgrau Nr.46. This was over-sprayed with Dunkelbraun Nr.45 in patches, so it covered roughly 1/3 of the Panzer.

Pz.Kpfw.II Ausf.A, B or C, 11.Panzer-Division, Ostfront 1941
Seen during the opening phase of Operation Barbarossa, this Panzer wears the Tac number, 42, in solid white characters on the turret sides; this number is probably repeated on the rear face as well. The unofficial, yet widely-used divisional insignia of the "Ghost Division" is seen on the sides of the superstructure, again in white, followed by a typical black/white Balkenkreuz. Both insignia were often seen on the hull's rear plate. Starting in June 1940, all new equipment was to be finished in a single color, Dunkelgrau RAL 7021; old equipment would have been re-painted as stocks became available and situation permitted.

Pz.Kpfw.II Ausf.F, 3.Kompanie, I.Abteilung, unidentified unit, Ostfront 1942
This Panzer was finished in a single color, Dunkelgrau RAL 7021; it has been given a rough covering of a lighter color, possibly one of the Tropen (tropical) colors that were issued beginning in 1941. It bears the tactical numbers, 345, in white outline form (designating it as belonging to 3.Kompanie, 4.Zug, Panzer number 5), on the sides of its turret; it is possibly repeated on the turret rear but the photographs on which this plate is based are inconclusive. A Balkenkreuz with a thick black center is surrounded by a thin white outline and is seen on each side of the superstructure, aft of the vision ports.

Pz.Kpfw.35(t), Panzer-Regiment 11, 1.leichte-Division, Poland 1939
Typical of Panzer from this unit, the large solid-white Balkenkreuze national insignia are seen on all four sides of the turret. A small rhomboid-shaped plate attached to the track-guards carried the three-digit Tac number, in this case, 533. This was often repeated on the rear face of the engine deck, again on a rhomboid-shaped plate. The base color was Dunkelgrau Nr.46. This was over-sprayed with Dunkelbraun Nr.45 in patches, so it covered roughly 1/3 of the Panzer.

Pz.Kpfw.38(t) Ausf.B, C or D, 1.Kompanie, I.Abteilung, 7. or 8.Panzer-Division, France 1940

This Panzer wears a Tac number, 134, on both sides of the turret; this is painted in white-outline form and shows a distinct color within the borders, which the author believes to be yellow. Typically, there is a broad white band painted on the engine deck as an aerial recognition device. A black/white Balkenkreuz is painted on the stowage lockers affixed to both sides of the track-guards; another would be seen on the hull rear plate. The base color of the Panzer is Dunkelgrau Nr.46. This is over-sprayed with Dunkelbraun Nr.45 in patches, so it covered roughly 1/3 of the Panzer.

Pz.Kpfw.38(t) Ausf.B, C or D, 2.Kompanie, I.Abteilung, 7. or 8.Panzer-Division, France 1940

Photographed crossing a bridge during the French Campaign, this Panzer sports a large three-digit Tac number, 215, on the turret side walls. The number is painted in white-outline form and shows a distinct color within the borders; the author believes the color to be yellow. A small rhomboid plate is seen at the rear of the engine deck; this would also have the Tac number painted upon it in white or yellow. A large white aerial recognition band is also seen painted laterally across the engine deck. The Balkenkreuze national insignia are black with a white outline and can be seen on the stowage locker on the port-side track-guard. The base color is Dunkelgrau Nr.46. This is over-sprayed with Dunkelbraun Nr.45 in patches, so it covers roughly 1/3 of the Panzer.

Pz.Kpfw.38(t) Ausf.B, C or D, 6.Kompanie, II.Abteilung, 7.Panzer-Division, France 1940
This Panzer carries very large, all-white three-digit Tac numbers, 621, on both sides of the turret. A large white aerial recognition band is also seen painted laterally across the engine deck. The Balkenkreuz national insignia is black with a white outline and can be seen on the stowage locker on the port-side track-guard. The division's insignia, an inverted "Y" followed by three dots is painted in yellow, just aft of the national insignia. The base color is Dunkelgrau Nr.46. This was over-sprayed with Dunkelbraun Nr.45 in patches, so it covered roughly 1/3 of the Panzer.

Pz.Kpfw.38(t) Ausf.B, C or D, 3.Kompanie, I.Abteilung, unidentified division, Ostfront 1941
This Panzer wears large Tac numbers, 352, in white-outline form, on the sides and rear of the turret. A black/white Balkenkreuz national insignia is seen on the large stowage locker fitted to the port-side track-guard. On the opposite side it could be seen on another locker (if fitted); otherwise it would be painted on the superstructure side plate. No unit insignia is visible; this Panzer was finished in a single color, Dunkelgrau RAL 7021.

A group of leichte Panzer (and a single early model Pz.Kpfw.III) holds a parade in a very unlikely winter setting; note the men at right of center standing in formation. Nearest the camera at far right is a Pz.Kpfw.I, identified by its characteristic front end mud-flap.

Crewmen belonging to a leichte Panzer-Kompanie stand ready for inspection in front of their Pz.Kpfw.IIs. All wear the standard M1935 Black AFV crew uniforms complete with oversized beret. Underneath their tunics they wear dark grey shirts with black ties, while their trousers are bloused over their standard jack-boots. These uniforms were worn in this fashion through the French Campaign of 1940, after which the beret and the padded helmet worn underneath were rarely seen; the impractical (for battle conditions) neck-tie soon followed suit.

A Pz.Kpfw.II Ausf.A or Ausf.B is parked nose-to-tail with a Pz.Kpfw.III Ausf.F, during the French Campaign of 1940. Note the extra road-wheels on the rear deck of the Pz.Kpfw.III and the fuel cans (jerry cans) on the engine decks of both Panzer; it is possible they are both in the process of being re-fueled. The rear faces of both turrets have the "Wolfsangle" (wolf trap) insignia of Panzer-Regiment 8, from 10.Panzer-Division painted in white. Each Panzer also has a series of bars on the rear face of their turrets (one vertical on the Pz.Kpfw.II and two horizontal on the Pz.Kpfw.III), which indicates their Kompanie affiliation.

A Pz.Kpfw.II fords a river probably during the French Campaign in 1940. Note that no apparent Balkenkreuz national insignia are visible; only white Tac numbers, 142, are seen on rhomboid plates on the superstructure sides and engine deck rear plate. This leichte Panzer also has a jerry can stowage rack similar to a photo of 4.Panzer-Division Pz.Kpfw.IIs, taken during the Polish Campaign in 1939, seen previously in this book.

A Pz.Kpfw.II Ausf.A or Ausf.B speeds by a stationary companion probably during the French Campaign of 1940. Both leichte Panzer have some of the modifications requested by the Panzertruppen after experiences in the Polish Campaign the previous year. These include Vorpanzer (spaced armor) on the bow and Zusatzpanzerung (appliqué armor) on the turret front and superstructure front. The moving Pz.Kpfw.II flies a Nazi flag from its rod antenna and is marked as belonging to the II.Abteilung's Stabs-Truppe (command group), in both large white-outline Tac numbers (II05) on the turret and smaller white numbers on the traditional rhomboid plate. The stationary Pz.Kpfw.II is marked as in the same fashion as belonging the 6.Kompanie (614), normally a constituent element of a Panzer-Regiment's II.Abteilung.

This photo of a pair of Pz.Kpfw.IIs, probably taken during the French Campaign of 1940, shows interesting markings on the leading leichte Panzer. Note the white oak-leaf on the front of the turret face, which was the unofficial insignia of 1.Panzer-Division. The white Tac numbers on the turret side, 111, have a small white dot following them, whose meaning is unknown to this author. The driver's visor on the leading Pz.Kpfw.II is different from that on the following Pz.Kpfw.II; this indicates they are Ausf.c and Ausf.A or Ausf.B, respectively.

A group of German Panzer crewmen pose on and near this Pz.Kpfw.II Ausf.c, probably during the French campaign of 1940; the lower case model designation is indicated by the configuration of the driver's view-port flap. This leichte Panzer has been modified with Vorpanzer (spaced armor) on the bow and Zusatzpanzerung (appliqué armor) on the turret front and superstructure front as a result of "lessons learned" during the previous years' conquest of Poland. Note also the three-digit white outline Tac number on the turret side walls, as well as the black/white Balkenkreuz national insignia on the superstructure side plate.

This photograph is unusual in that it shows the Notek black-out driving head-lamp mounted on the port side track-guard of a Pz.Kpfw.II Ausf.A, B or C obviously somewhere in France as denoted by the café sign on the building in the background. Whether this image was made during the actual campaign itself is open to conjecture since the leichte Panzer is devoid of any stowage on the usually cluttered bow. Note the Vorpanzer (spaced armor) on the bow and Zusatzpanzerung (appliqué armor) on the turret front and superstructure front; the commander's hatch lid is the original two-piece design.

A previous photograph in this book depicted a Pz.Kpfw.I next to this bunker complex; here we see several more, joined by some Pz.Kpfw.IIs. Note the absence of the swing-out anti-aircraft machine-gun mount on the near side of both Pz.Kpfw.IIs as well as the relative lack of any visible markings, except rhomboid plates for Tac numbers.

This Pz.Kpfw.II has all of the recommended post-1939 upgrades in place. Note the new commander's cupola with periscopes around the rim, Vorpanzer (spaced armor) on the bow, Zusatzpanzerung (appliqué armor) on the turret front and superstructure and the Notek black-out driving head-lamp on the port side track-guard.

When first shipped to North Africa in early 1941, German Panzer of 5.leichte-Division wore their European camouflage scheme, in this case it was overall Dunkelgrau RAL 7021. Large, white-outline three-digit Tac numbers also featured on these Panzer, which were taken from Panzer-Regiment 5 of 3.Panzer-Division. This Pz.Kpfw.II Ausf.A, B or C carries numbers designating it as the 2nd Panzer of the 3rd Zug (platoon) of the 4.Kompanie, I.Abteilung. It would appear that all of the desired modifications have been carried out on this Panzer; they include Zusatzpanzer (appliqué armor panels) on the superstructure front and the turret front and Vorpanzer (spaced armor) on the bow. The new commander's cupola featured all around vision using periscopes set about the rim and it now has a smaller single circular hatch lid. Note the rack of jerry cans on the turret roof, another common feature of these early DAK (Deutsches Afrika Korps) Panzer.

After experiences in the Polish Campaign of 1939, several modifications to the Pz.Kpfw.II were requested by the Panzertruppen. Among these modifications were added stowage lockers to be mounted on the track-guards and a circular commander's cupola with periscopes and a single-piece hatch lid; both are seen here applied to an Ausf.A or Ausf.B (which is identified as such by the configuration of the driver's view-port flaps). Zusatzpanzerung (appliqué armor) was to be fitted to the turret and superstructure front plates, while Vorpanzer (spaced armor) was to be fitted to the bow; neither of these modifications are present here. Note the divisional insignia, an upright "Y" with one vertical stroke, in yellow, on the superstructure front plate next to the driver's vision port-flap. This was used by 8.Panzer-Division during Operation Barbarossa beginning in June 1941, which is presumably where this image was made.

These vehicles are from the Stabs-Kompanie (headquarters company) of II.Abteilung (as signified by the white Roman numeral "II" on the turrets), Panzer-Regiment.10, 8.Panzer-Division and are seen during the early stages of Operation Barbarossa. In the foreground is a Pz.Kpfw.II Ausf.A, B or C that has the addition of a large stowage bin on the fender, circular commander's cupola with periscopes on the turret, Zusatzpanzer (appliqué armor panels) on the superstructure front and the turret front and finally Vorpanzer (spaced armor) on the bow. The yellow divisional sign, an upright "Y" with a single vertical tick mark next to its base is just visible in front of the "II". A Pz.Kpfw.38(t) with similar markings is in the background; note that both Panzer are well dispersed and use the defilade of the terrain for protection against enemy observation or fire.

This Pz.Kpfw.II Ausf.C of the 11.Panzer-Division has also been modified with all items requested after the completion of the Polish Campaign. These include Vorpanzer (spaced armor) on the bow and Zusatzpanzerung (appliqué armor) on the turret front and superstructure front. The new commander's cupola that had a round, single-piece hatch lid and periscopes around the rim has also been installed as has been the Notek black-out driving head-lamp on the port side track-guard. The large new-pattern stowage locker has also been fitted on the starboard side track-guard. This leichte Panzer is marked with the division's un-official ghost insignia on the superstructure side plate; it appears that the official insignia, a ring bisected by a vertical bar on the superstructure front plate has been over-painted. A two-digit Tac number in white, 42, is seen on the turret side wall; forward of and below this appears to be an over-painted Panzer rhomboid, which, along with the two-digit number was also a typical marking seen on this division's Panzer.

Eerily similar to an earlier photograph in this book, a column of Pz.Kpfw.IIs (the first and second are Ausf.Cs; the third is an Ausf.c) moves along a tree-lined village road, possibly during the opening stages of Operation Barbarossa in June 1941. Note that the two leading leichte Panzer have the Vorpanzer (spaced armor) on the bow and Zusatzpanzerung (appliqué armor) on the turret front and superstructure front. In addition, they have all been modified with a new commander's cupola that had a round, single-piece hatch lid and periscopes around the rim. Notek black-out driving head-lamps are also seen on the port side track-guards; although authorized long before, these were seldom seen on German AFVs prior to the campaigns of 1941.

Pz.Kpfw.38(t) of a Panzer-Kompaine deploy while several Pz.Kpfw.IIs (Ausf.A, B or C) remain in place in a photograph probably made during the opening phases of Operation Barbarossa in June 1941. Note that the Pz.Kpfw.IIs have the Vorpanzer (spaced armor) on the bow and Zusatzpanzerung (appliqué armor) on the turret front and superstructure front. The new commander's cupola that had a round, single-piece hatch lid and periscopes around the rim has also been installed as has been the Notek black-out driving head-lamp on the port side track-guard. In addition, the first leichte Panzer in the column has been fitted with triple smoke candle launchers on the rear of the track-guards. While no markings are visible on any of the Panzer, the motorcycle combination at right has a white "J" (actually equivalent to the letter "I") on the rear of the side-car. This denotes it as belonging to the Instandstruppe, or maintenance section.

A Pz.Kpfw.II Ausf.A, B or C crosses a small engineer bridge, probably during the drive into the Soviet Union during the opening phases of Opertaion Barbarossa. It features some of the modifications requested after the Polish Campaign, including Vorpanzer (spaced armor) on the bow and Zusatzpanzerung (appliqué armor) on the turret front and superstructure front. The new commander's cupola has not been fitted, but a Notek black-out driving head-lamp has been mounted on the port side track-guard.

A pair of dust-covered Pz.Kpfw.IIs (Ausf.A, B or C) crosses an open field. Both have all of the requested modifications including: Notek black-out driving head-lamp on the port side track-guard, Vorpanzer (spaced armor) on the bow and Zusatzpanzerung (appliqué armor) on the turret front and superstructure front, commander's cupola with round, single-piece hatch lid and periscopes around the rim and stowage locker on the starboard side track-guard. There is a black/white Balkenkreuz national insignia on the stowage locker, and there is also a rhomboid plate attached to the stowage box behind it, with a white Tac number, possibly "402". Note the unusual, unidentified item on the near leichte Panzer's engine deck.

Smoke rises in the distance as curious Germans wonder what it means. The Pz.Kpfw.II in the immediate foreground has a Nazi flag for use as an aerial recognition device and also carries a 200-liter fuel drum on the engine deck. Note also the triple smoke grenade dischargers on the starboard side track-guard.

German infantrymen huddle in the lee of a Pz.Kpfw.II for protection from enemy fire. This leichte Panzer has a Nebelkerzenabwurfvorrichtung (rack to deploy smoke candles) on the rear plate over the exhaust muffler. Note also the black/white Balkenkreuz national insignia of the rear plate of the superstructure.

A pair of Pz.Kpfw.IIs (Ausf.A, B or C) lead several Pz.Kpfw.38(t)s during the campaign on the Ostfront. Both leichte Panzer have been fitted with Vorpanzer (spaced armor) on the bow, Zusatzpanzerung (appliqué armor) on the turret front and superstructure, new commander's cupola and Notek black-out driving head-lamps. The second Pz.Kpfw.II carries the insignia of 12.Panzer-Division (a circle divided in three parts) on the superstructure front plate. What appears to be two dots on the superstructure side plate of the lead vehicle, is actually a black/white Balkenkreuz that has been foreshortened due to the camera angle.

48

A Pz.kpfw.II Ausf.A, B or C brings up the rear of a column somewhere on the vast steppes of the Soviet Union. Visible in this photo is the retro-fitted commander's cupola; it can be assumed that Vorpanzer (spaced armor) has been fitted the bow and that Zusatzpanzerung (appliqué armor) has been fitted on the turret front and superstructure. This leichte Panzer is part of an Abteilung's command group as attested by the white-outline Tac marking (II5) on the rear face of the turret; note also the black/white Balkenkreuz national insignia on the rear plate of the hull.

Seen somewhere on the Ostfront, several German AFVs have dispersed as a counter to an on-going enemy artillery barrage. Two leichte Panzer, a pair of mittlerer Schützenpanzerwagen Sd.Kfz.251s and a Befhelspanzer III Ausf.H can be seen. In the center of the photo stands a Pz.Kpfw.II (Ausf.A, B or C), with all of the mandated modifications including Vorpanzer (spaced armor) on the bow, Zusatzpanzerung (appliqué armor) on the turret front and superstructure, new commander's cupola and Notek blackout driving head-lamps. The two radio antennae and the cupola identify the Pz.Kpfw.III as a Befhelspanzer III Ausf.H. Note also the dummy 5cm gun on the mantle as well as the ball-mounted MG34.

49

On the Ostfront, the so-called "road network" usually consisted of beaten tracks that were dusty when dry and a sea of mud when wet. In this instance a German truck has come to grief on a rutted road, and is being hauled out by any available means, in this case a Pz.Kpfw.II Ausf.A, B or C. The leichte Panzer has been fitted with the modification package which included Vorpanzer (spaced armor) on the bow, Zusatzpanzerung (appliqué armor) on the turret and superstructure front plates, new commander's cupola, enlarged stowage locker on the starboard side track-guard, and Notek black-out driving head-lamps. Note the large white letter "G" on the lower bow plate; this identifier was applied to many vehicles that belonged to Panzergruppe Guderian.

This Pz.Kpfw.II from 2.Panzer-Division (note the two yellow dots just forward of the Balkenkreuz on the superstructure side plate) is undergoing extensive field maintenance. The engine deck has been removed, with the Maybach HL62TR engine lifted out for ease of access to various parts of it. The 2cm KwK and 7.92mm MG34 have also been removed from the turret. Note the Vorpanzer (spaced armor) on the bow (with a crewman standing in the open hatch) and Zusatzpanzerung (appliqué armor) on the turret front and superstructure. This leichte Panzer retains the original split hatch lids on the turret roof; the later commander's cupola has not been fitted.

Several Pz.Kpfw.IIs, backed up by a Pz.Kpfw.IV, have halted for a maintenance break. Note that the nearest leichte Panzer (an Ausf.A, B or C) has the Vorpanzer (spaced armor) on the bow and Zusatzpanzerung (appliqué armor) on the turret front and superstructure, but retains the original split hatch lids on the turret roof. It wears a white two-digit Tac number, 31, on the turret side as well as a black/white Balkenkreuz on the superstructure side plate. Finally, it has lost the rod antenna storage trough normally seen mounted to the port side track-guard.

This pair of images possibly depicts a Pz.Kpfw.II Ausf.F as it stands in for a background for a group photograph of several infantrymen. It is thought to be that particular model due to the appearance of the later idler wheel without radial spokes. It wears a white-outline three digit Tac number, 345 on the side of the turret; below on the superstructure side is a Balkenkreuz national insignia. A rough hand-applied disruptive camouflage pattern has been applied, probably using one of the colors designed for use on Panzer that were shipped to hot-weather climates, such as Southern Russia and North Africa. The Pz.Kpfw.II series was the only German-produced Panzer to have the radio antenna and its protective trough situated on the port-side track-guard; all others had this fitting on the starboard side.

These two images provide two angles of the same Pz.Kpfw.II Ausf.F. It is identified as an Ausf.F by the straight superstructure front plate, the retention of the five road-wheels with spring bundles for the suspension, the return rollers, track links with pairs of edge-mounted guide horns, drive sprocket with single toothed ring and later style idler wheel. The head-on view shows battle damage on the starboard track-guard and stowage locker, while the side view shows a Tac number on the turret, probably 231.

A column of German Panzer is interspersed with an Opel Blitz 3-ton truck and a motorcycle combination, somewhere on the Ostfront. The Panzer are Pz.Kpfw.II Ausf.D chassis' converted into Panzerkampfwagen II (Flamm) (Sd.Kfz.122). The normal turret with 2cm KwK and 7.92mm MG34 was replaced by a fixed casemate mounting a single MG34 and vision devices. Two Spritzeköpfe (spray heads), one on each forward end of the track-guards, could send a stream of fire or flame oil out to a distance of about 30-meters, with a favorable wind.

A Flammpanzer II Ausf.D passes between a group of communications specialists who are holding a field telephone wire up out of harm's way using rods. The near Panzer has been garnished with foliage to break up its outline; it is followed at a proper tactical interval by a sister vehicle. These specialized Flammpanzer served with two units on the Ostfront, Pz.Abt.(F)100 and Pz.Abt.(F)101, from 1941. By early 1942, both units had been converted back to standard Panzer-Abteilungen.

The Pz.Kpfw.II Ausf.D and Ausf.E featured a new torsion-bar suspension system instead of the leaf-spring bundles seen up through the Ausf.C and the later Ausf.F. Note the four (instead of five seen previously) road-wheels, and the new drive sprocket, which drove a new track that had center guide horns; there were no return rollers. Un-lubricated tracks, as seen here, denoted the Ausf.D chassis. The armored boxes on either track-guard held nitrogen cylinders for propelling the flame oil; the oil was ignited using acetylene also from pressurized cylinders. Note the mini-turrets that housed the flame projecting Spritzeköpfe (spray heads); the crew has also stored cylinders of compressed nitrogen or acetylene on top of the armored housings.

This head-on view provides an excellent view of the various vision devices seen on the Flammpanzer II Ausf.D The view-ports for the driver and radio operator are identical to each other and were also carried over to the later Pz.Kpfw.II Ausf.F as well as the Marder II. The two ports on either side of the fixed casemate are similar to those seen on Pz.Kpfw.IIIs and Pz.Kpfw.IVs with 30mm armor. The Kugelblende (ball mount) for the MG34 was a standard fitting and was also seen on Pz.Kpfw.IIIs and Pz.Kpfw.IVs with 30mm armor. Note the triple-tube Nebelwurfgerät (smoke candle dischargers) on the rear of the port-side track guard; presumably a like installation was seen on the opposite side.

Another head-on view of a different Flammpanzer II Ausf.D shows that it is similarly-configured to the previous Panzer. Note the black-out covers with slits placed over the conventional head-lamps. A Notek black-out driving head-lamp is fitted on the center of the glacis plate and a triple-tube Nebelwurfgerät (smoke candle dischargers) appears on the rear of the starboard-side track guard; again, an identical installation should be seen on the opposite side.

A rear view of a pair of Flammpanzer II Ausf.Ds allows the modeler to see several details of the type. The small rectangular device on the port-side of the rear plate is a convoy distance marker tail-lamp; it was usually fitted as part of the Notek black-out driving system. The long thin apparatus low on the hull rear plate is the exhaust muffler; above it is an air deflector associated with the engine cooling system. The Nebelkerzenabwurfvorrichtung (rack to deploy smoke candles) has an armored cover which has been marked with a white-outline Balkenkreuz national insignia as well as a rhomboid shape with a number indicating the Kompanie to which the Flammpanzer was attached. Note also the second Balkenkreuz on the casemate rear faces of both vehicles and the bundles of fascines on the port-side track guards. As these Flammpanzer were designed to assault fortifications, the fascine bundles would come in handy to fill in any anti-tank ditches that were placed so as to hinder them.

A total of 29 Panzerspähwagen II (2cm) (Sd.Kfz.123) Lüchs (Lynx) were issued to 2.Kompanie/Panzer-Aufklärungs-Abteilung 4 of 4.Panzer-Division beginning in early 1943, where they served initially on the Ostfront. This Lüchs carries common stowage and modifications seen fitted to vehicles of this unit. This includes a rack over the edge of the superstructure roof plate holding replaceable inserts for the idler wheel rim as well as a plate spaced away from the bow armor; curved front mud-flaps were also common on these early machines. Triple Nebelwurfgerät (smoke candle dischargers) are mounted on either side of the turret; these were later officially dispensed with, but were often still seen in use.

Another Panzerspähwagen II (2cm) (Sd.Kfz.123) Lüchs (Lynx) from 4.Panzer-Division has stowage features nearly identical to those seen in the previous image. These include the rack to store spare idler wheel rim segments, added spaced plate on the bow and triple Nebelwurfgerät (smoke candle dischargers) are mounted on either front corner of the turret. This Lüchs has both curved mud-flaps hinged to the track-guards, a large stowage locker on the port-side and vehicle width indicator rods on both sides, outboard of the Bosch black-out driving head-lamps.

Seen moving across a snowy Ostfront landscape, this Panzerspähwagen II (2cm) (Sd.Kfz.123) Lüchs (Lynx) from 4.Panzer-Division again shows stowage arrangements and modifications typical of this unit. At this stage, the curved front mud-flaps are gone from the track-guards but the spaced plate on the bow is still retained as are the pair of triple Nebelwurfgerät (smoke candle dischargers) mounted on the front corners of the turret. Idler wheel segments are stowed on the forward edge of the superstructure and spare track links are seen on the glacis plate. The sole visible marking is the Balkenkreuz seen on the stowage locker on the near side track-guard.

When Germany annexed Czechoslovakia in 1938, it gained access to a modern arms production industry, which included tank production facilities, such as the Skoda plant. One of their recent products was the LT vz.35 light tank, which had recently gone into production; all extant vehicles were confiscated by Germany, who initially designated them as the Pz.Kpfw. L.T.Sk.35. Chassis number 13692, still in its original Czech factory-applied camouflage is seen here being inspected by a group of Heer (Army) non-commissioned officers.

A German Panzer crewman adjusts his clothing while a trio of Pz.Kpfw. L.T.Sk.35s awaits his attention. Note that the nearest Panzer has a German vehicle jack laying on the track-guard; also of interest is the protruding stowage locker that was integrated into the front-most bogie wheel assembly. All visible Panzer wear their Czech camouflage colors, while the one in the center of the photo also retains the original five-digit registration numbers on the rear plate.

These two photographs depict the same Panzerkampfwagen (3.7cm) L.T.Sk.35 (as the Panzer was referred to at the time of the Polish Campaign in 1939) from 1.leichte-Division. The Panzer has been re-finished in the standard German color scheme consisting of Dunkelgrau Nr.46 over-painted with Dunkelbraun Nr.45; it also wears the wide all-white Balkenkreuz national insignia on the turret, which would be seen on all four vertical surfaces. A white, three-digit Tac number, 533 is seen painted onto a rhomboid plate, which itself is attached to the track-guards by a stalk; a similar device would be seen on the rear plate of the Panzer.

Parked on the side of a Polish street, one of a pair of Panzerkampfwagen (3.7cm) L.T.Sk.35s gets the "once-over" by a group of curious German troops. It is clearly seen how prominent the white Balkenkreuze national insignia were when viewed against the dark colors of the Panzer of the era. This led to over-painting in the field and a change to the insignia after the campaign's end.

A crew struggles to free their bogged-down Panzerkampfwagen (3.7cm) L.T.Sk.35 from soft forest ground. It can again be seen how prominent the Balkenkreuze national insignia could be, even in the shadows of the trees.

This damaged Panzerkampfwagen (3.7cm) L.T.Sk.35 sits upon a Sd.Ah.115 trailer as it is hauled to workshops for repair. Note the damage to the far track-guard as well as the loss of the mount for the radio operator's 7.92mm MG37(t). Aside from the usual Balkenkreuze national insignia seen on all vertical surfaces of the turret, the three-digit Tac number, 221, is seen on the typical rhomboid plate on the near-side track-guard.

This non-descript Pz.Kpfw.35(t) moves along a hill-side, probably during a training exercise. A registration number, possibly 13476, is painted in black, low on the bow plate. Note the cover over the muzzle of the 3.7cm KwK(t) and the lack of flash suppressors on both 7.92mm MG37(t)s.

Prior to the French Campaign of 1940, Pz.Kpfw.35(t)s (as they were now designated) had their Balkenkreuz national insignia changed to a style that featured a thin white outline with a black core. Their position was also changed to three places on the hull/superstructure, instead of the previous four places on the turret. This pair of Panzer belonging to 6.Panzer-Division, are parked on the side of a street next to some local structures, during winter exercises.

Although difficult to place with any certainty, this Pz.Kpfw.35(t) is probably seen during the French Campaign of 1940. Note the additional rack on the engine deck for 20-liter jerrycans and the rhomboid plate with a white Tac number, 212, just below the rack. The rear hull plate features a black/white Balkenkreuz national insignia, while the Tac numbers are also repeated on the turret sides and rear.

A pair of Pz.Kpfw.35(t)s takes a rest on the side of a road as wheeled vehicles pass, during the French Campaign of 1940. Note the white letter "G" (for Guderian) painted on the windshield of the near car and the white-outline Balkenkreuz on the superstructure side plate of the near Panzer. The only unit operating the Pz.Kpfw.35(t) in 1940 was the 6.Panzer-Division, which, like Guderian's XIX Panzer-Korps, was subordinated to Panzergruppe von Kleist. The far Panzer features various racks for 20-liter jerrycans on the near track-guard and engine deck; these racks were virtually the only modifications made by the Germans. Finally, the far Panzer sports a Nazi party flag as an aerial recognition device.

The vastness of the terrain indicates that these Panzer, including the Pz.Kpfw.35(t) at right, are operating on the Ostfront during the opening phases of operation Barbarossa in the summer of 1941. The Pz.Kpfw.35(t) was used as a substitute for the Pz.kpfw.III medium tank in the single German unit, 6.Panzer-Division, which used the type during the campaign; note the Pz.Kpfw.IVs in the background.

A Pz.Kpfw.38(t) of undetermined model is covered in troops, probably at a driver's training center. Note that the 3.7cm KwK(t) has not been fitted and that a Notek black-out driving head-lamp can be seen just over the front edge of the near-side track-guard. The lack of armament suggests that this is a Fahrschulepanzer.

A group of German troops are briefed by their NCOs as they stand next to a Pz.Kpfw.38(t) Ausf.B, C or D. The Panzer carries no armament but has been retro-fitted with a Notek black-out driving head-lamp in the usual place on the port side track-guard; this suggests that this pristine vehicle is being used for training. A black/white Balkenkreuz national insignia is seen on the superstructure side plate, while an alphanumeric designation, S71, is seen on the turret's side wall on what is probably a Fahrschulepanzer.

61

The four-man crew of this Pz.Kpfw.38(t) Ausf.B, C or D als Zugfr.Wg. (platoon commander's vehicle) pose with some friends for posterity. Note the circular plate over the radio operator's position where the 7.92mm MG37(t) has been removed to make room for additional radio gear in its stead. The Notek black-out driving head-lamp has been fitted on the port side edge of the glacis plate. Spare track links can be seen fitted to the bow and glacis plates on the standard racks, while more are seen on the starboard side track-guard.

Another brightly-marked Pz.Kpfw.38(t) Ausf.B, C or D serves as a background for some of its crew-members and several other men, possibly prior to the French Campaign of 1940. Note the large Tac numbers, 621, on the turret side as well as the black/white Balkenkreuz on the track-guard-mounted stowage locker; aft of the cross is the insignia of 7.Panzer-Division, an inverted "Y" followed by three dots (with the third covered by one of the men), in yellow. Finally, a large white rectangle has been painted on the engine deck as an aerial recognition device.

The crew of this Pz.Kpfw.38(t) Ausf.E/F als Zugfr.Wg poses for the camera, probably at their home station. The bolt pattern on the turret front indicates that this Panzer has a sandwich of two 25mm armor plates on the front, which was a principal feature of the Ausf. E and Ausf.F; the circular blanking plate over the area where the 7.92mm MG37(t) was mounted designates this as a platoon, company, or battalion command tank. Note the two sets of Tac numbers on the turret side walls, an "11" followed by a larger "7". Other details of interest are the commander's rotating periscope on the turret roof, the shrouded rear-view mirror on the front end of the track-guard, the rod antenna on its rubber base and the factory-standard stowage of a tow cable and shovel further aft.

This brightly-marked and relatively clean Pz.Kpfw.38(t) Ausf.B, C or D makes its way out of its hull-down position, possibly just prior to the French Campaign in 1940. Note again the large three-digit Tac number, 134, on the side of the turret; it would again appear that the fill color is far lighter than red or black. A black/white Balkenkreuz is seen on the track-guard mounted stowage locker and there is a prominent white rectangle painted on the engine deck as an aerial recognition device.

A schwere Zugkraftwagen 18-ton Sd.Kfz.9 hauls a Sd.Ah.115 tank transport trailer topped with a Pz.Kpfw.38(t) Ausf.B, C or D across an engineer pontoon bridge during the French Campaign of 1940. The position of the exhaust muffler denotes the model of this Panzer, while the style of markings and locale indicates the probable area of operations. It is this author's contention that the Tac numbers, 215, are yellow, outlined in white. Note the standard black/white Balkenkreuz on the stowage locker on the near track-guard; there is also a white rectangle painted on the engine deck, beneath the stowage box, which was used as an aerial recognition device.

This Pz.Kpfw.38(t) Ausf.B, C or D lies destroyed and partially stripped somewhere in France during the 1940 campaign. Note the remnants of a three-digit Tac number on the turret side wall and a white-outline Balkenkreuz on the near-side superstructure. The tracks have been disconnected and the drive sprocket has been removed.

A column of Pz.Kpfw.38(t) Ausf.B, C or Ds make their way through a rain-soaked French village during the 1940 campaign. Note that the commander of the nearest Panzer wears his Zeltbahn camouflage rain cape and that there is a three-digit Tac number, 534, on the typical rhomboid plate attached to the engine deck. A white-outline Balkenkreuz is seen to the right of the Tac number plate, while a shovel and tow cable has been re-located by the unit to the hull rear plate.

A disabled Pz.Kpfw.38(t) Ausf.B, C or D lies on the side of a road some time during or immediately after the French Campaign of 1940. Some un-armed German soldiers on commandeered civilian bicycles (apparently out for a joy-ride in the country) are examining the Panzer, which has been stripped of any loose items while it awaits recovery.

This Pz.Kpfw.38(t) Ausf.B, C or D shows some interesting markings, such as a rhomboid shape painted on the turret rear wall, a three-digit Tac number, 323, on a plate attached to the engine deck, and a white-outline Balkenkreuz beside it. Many units modified tool stowage arrangements, as seen here; note that the shovel and tow cable, normally seen on the superstructure side plate has been moved to the rear hull plate. The track-guards have been fitted with bundles of fascines as well as various stowage lockers, while a five-cell Nebelkerzenabwurfvorrichtung (rack to deploy smoke candles) has been fitted over the exhaust muffler.

Two crew-members of this Pz.Kpfw.38(t) Ausf.B, C or D converse while their Panzer is halted on the road-side. Note the bundle of fascines on the track-guard and the re-located shovel and tow-cable, now seen on the hull rear plate. This dusty vehicle shows no markings except for a three-digit Tac marking, 532, on a rhomboid plate attached to the engine deck.

This Pz.Kpfw.38(t) Ausf.B, C or D is seen during the opening stages of Operation Barbarossa in June of 1941, as it makes its way into Stalin's Soviet Union. Note the tapered tube on the horn as well as the Notek black-out driving head-lamp on the far and near track-guards, respectively. A white-outline three-digit Tac number, 352, has been painted on the turret side wall, while a black/white Balkenkreuz national insignia is seen on the track-guard-mounted stowage locker. As all weapons are covered for protection from the ever-pervasive mid-summer dust, combat does not appear imminent.

This heavily-stowed and dusty Pz.Kpfw.38(t) Ausf.G has paused on the side of the road for a photograph. It is identified as an Ausf.G by the bolt pattern on the forward edge of the turret and the single piece of 50mm armor on the front plate. A series of stowage lockers have been fitted to the near-side track guard and the Panzer has been partially covered with foliage in order to break up its outline. Note the position of the Notek black-out driving head-lamp on the edge of the glacis plate (another Ausf.G feature) and the location of the fire extinguisher on the far track-guard.

This mud-spattered Pz.Kpfw.38(t) Ausf. E, F or G leads a group of wheeled vehicles on a road, possibly during the opening phases of Operation Barbarossa. The light field car is a Stoewer or BMW, while the other vehicle is an Opel Blitz 3-ton truck. The Panzer has a stowage locker as well as a rack holding a bundle of wired-together saplings on the near track-guard; the latter was used to help negotiate soft ground. A Nazi flag, used as an aerial recognition device is hung, tent-like over the engine deck, while a smaller pennant is fixed to a small staff next to the commander's cupola.

This burned-out 8.Kompanie Pz.Kpfw.38(t) Ausf.B, C or D has seen better days! The turret sports large three-digit Tac numbers, 811 on the side walls; the rear Tac number is painted on a field-applied Gepäckkasten (baggage bin). The perforated stowage locker seen on the track-guards has been re-located aft; just forward of that is what is probably a rack for a 20-liter jerry can. A Notek black-out driving head-lamp has been fitted to the front end of the port side track-guard; thus it is likely that this Panzer was destroyed on the Ostfront.

It is possible that these two photographs depict the same Pz.Kpfw.38(t) Ausf.B, C or D (identified by the bolt pattern on the turret front plate for 25mm armor) from 12.Panzer-Division (note the division's insignia, a yellow ring divided in three, on the far corner of the superstructure front plate) on the Ostfront in 1941. Note the stowage bin arrangement, the location of the Tac number, 322 (hidden in one image) and the peculiar circular fitting on the third road-wheel. The armament is covered with canvas shrouds to keep out the elements and a large amount of stowage, including steel helmets festoons the Panzer.

This Pz.Kpfw.38(t) of an undetermined Ausführung (model) has been loaded onto a railroad flat-car for its trip to what is probably the Ostfront. There is a chalked-on number on the bow plate, which is obscured by the crewmen; this may be the chassis number, which was often applied at the factory prior to issue to a receiving unit. Note the Notek black-out driving head-lamp on the port side track-guard and the overall clean appearance of this Panzer.

A column of Panzer, led by a Pz.Kpfw.38(t) Ausf.B, C or D, moves out along a road that has been paved with small stones. This dusty and otherwise non-descript Panzer has a Notek black-out driving head-lamp mounted on the port side track-guard.

A thoroughly dust-covered Pz.Kpfw.38(t) Ausf.B, C or D, followed by a schwerer Panzerspähwagen (8-Rad) Sd.Kfz.231, leads a column of wheeled vehicles through the mud of a "road" on the Ostfront. The Panzer is identified as an Ausf.B, C or D by the stepped front plate on the superstructure; note the unusual stowage of a road-wheel on the glacis plate.

A Pz.Kpfw.38(t) of an undetermined Ausführung (model) does duty as a tractor at a river crossing by pulling trucks through the mud. Note how the surrounding terrain has been turned into a quagmire by the still-evident melting snows; this spring thaw heralded the coming of the infamous Russian "Rasputitsa" mud.

While the driver pilots his Panzer, the remaining crewmembers of this Pz.Kpfw.38(t) Ausf.B, C or D ride outside to get some fresh air. Once they reached the user unit, most of these Panzer had their stowage modified so that extra lockers could be mounted on the track-guards, as seen here. This unit has applied a black/white Balkenkreuze as well as a three-digit Tac number, 223, in yellow, to the near-side locker.

Sited next to a rail-head, this Pz.Kpfw.38(t) Ausf. B, C or D (identified by the bolt pattern on the turret front plate for 25mm armor) is either awaiting fuel or providing site security somewhere on the Ostfront, probably in 1942. Its stowage and markings pattern resemble that seen on Panzer of 12.Panzer-Division, while the crew has also stowed their water bottles on the turret exterior. A tray for 20-liter jerrycans is fitted to the engine deck; this was first seen during the French Campaign of 1940.

This Pz.Kpfw.38(t) Ausf. B, C or D (identified by the bolt pattern on the turret front plate for 25mm armor) raises a cloud of dust as it leads a Pz.Kpfw.II Ausf.A, B or C and a Pz.Kpfw.IV down an incline. This Panzer has not had extensive stowage modifications made to it, nor does it exhibit much in the way of extra gear hanging about; additionally, no markings are visible.

This Pz.Kpfw.38(t) Ausf. E, F or G is identified from this angle by the raised exhaust muffler, first introduced on the Ausf.E. Just below the muffler is the armored box containing a bank of Nebelkerzenabwurfvorrichtung (rack to deploy smoke candles). This image also affords an excellent insight into how German Pioniertruppen would prepare ditches for crossing by motorized transport and AFVs. Note the logs placed at right angles across the earth and stone road-bed; other logs are laid at a 90-degree angle atop them to provide a hard surface for vehicular traffic.

A Pz.Kpfw.38(t) Ausf.G moves along a snow-covered track somewhere on the Ostfront; the placement of the Notek black-out driving head-lamp on the glacis identifies the model. It has been white-washed for concealment against the snow and there is a dark spot on the side of the turret, which is a partial view of a Tac number. A road-wheel has been stored on the bow, with the back-side out so it acts as a stowage tray for cables and other paraphernalia.

Raising a tactically un-sound cloud of dust as it moves at speed, this Pz.Kpfw.38(t) can be identified as an Ausf. E or F by the configuration of the radio operator's visor flap on the superstructure's front plate. This Panzer has a Notek black-out driving head-lamp on the port side track-guard, which likely precludes it being an Ausf.G since the latter had this feature moved to the glacis plate. To escape the heat of a summer on the Ostfront (probably that of 1942) all of the crew except the driver are sitting outside, or in the case of the commander, "head-out" of his cupola.

Although the weather is not pleasant, the crew of this Pz.Kpfw.38(t) Ausf. E, F or G (identified by the configuration of the radio operator's visor on the superstructure front plate) poses merrily with some friends. This Panzer has a large stowage locker on the port side track-guard, which has a black/white Balkenkreuze national insignia on it; the frontal aspect seems to be covered in a white-wash winter camouflage. Note also the protruding pipe from the exhaust muffler at the rear; its height is also indicative of the Ausf.E, F or G.

As the war progressed, the Pz.Kpfw.38(t) became obsolete as a front-line Panzer. Those that survived the meat-grinder that was the Ostfront were eventually relegated to less demanding tasks, such as providing security for rear-area troops. In this case, what is probably an Ausf.E or F is covering a group of telephone line-men as they use their typical poles to hang wire on the trees of this avenue. The tranquil scene (note two curious local boys) shows no trace of combat, while the paved streets and architecture suggest an Eastern European location, possibly Poland or Czechoslovakia. Note the small infantry cart in the foreground.

This Pz.Kpfw.38(t) Ausf.E or F als Zugfr.Wg (identified by the radio operator's visor and blanking plate over the former 7.92mm MG37(t) mount on the superstructure front plate) appears to be providing security for the pair of troop-laden Opel Blitz 3-ton trucks seen on the streets of a German-occupied city. Note the stowage locker (in this instance, the perforated front end is shown) and the bundle of wired-together saplings on the port side track-guard.

Perched atop his cupola's hatch lid, this commander of a Pz.Kpfw.38(t) Ausf.E or F (note the superstructure front plate's rivet pattern) takes in the sunny summer weather on the Ostfront. The Panzer has been fitted with a typical stowage locker on the track-guard and the crew has also hung their steel helmets on the turret side wall. Most models of the Pz.Kpfw.38(t) had small eyelets attached to various rivet heads located on the turret and superstructure; these had wire or rope threaded through them to which gear (or camouflage material) could be affixed.

This Panzerbefehlswagen 38(t) Ausf.E or F has the blanking plate over the former mount for the radio operator's 7.92mm MG37(t) as well as the characteristic (and conspicuous) Rahmenantenne (frame antenna) for the long range Fu.5 and Fu.8 radio set, making it an Sd.Kfz.267 as used by the Panzer-Regiment's Stabskompanie (headquarters company). Among the stowage items seen on the bow is a length of track and a 20-liter jerry can, while a large locker has been mounted to the starboard side track-guard.